Archaeology of the Teufelsberg

For over 50 years, the white radomes of the Teufelsberg have been one of Berlin's most prominent landmarks. For half of this time the city lay over 100mi behind an 'Iron Curtain' that divided East from West, and was surrounded by communist East Germany and the densest concentration of Warsaw Pact military forces in Europe. From the vantage point high on the Teufelsberg, British and American personnel constantly monitored the electronic emissions from the surrounding military forces, as well as high-level political intelligence. Today, the Teufelsberg stands as a contemporary and spectacular ruin, representing a significant relic of a lost cyber space of Cold War electronic emissions and espionage. Based on archaeological fieldwork and recently declassified documents, this book presents a new history of the Teufelsberg and other Western intelligence gathering sites in Berlin. At a time when intelligence gathering is once more under close scrutiny, when questions are being asked about the intelligence relationship between the United States and Russia and amidst wider debate about the US's National Security Agency (NSA) intelligence programmes, sites like the Teufelsberg raise questions that appear both important and timely.

Wayne D Cocroft is an archaeologist and manager of Historic England's Historic Places Investigation Team East based in Cambridge. For over 25 years he has specialised in the investigation and assessment of former military sites, including explosives factories and Cold War research and development establishments. His published works include *Dangerous energy: the archaeology of gunpowder and military explosives manufacture*, and he has also co-authored *Cold War: building for nuclear confrontation 1946–1989* and *War art: murals and graffiti – military life, power and subversion*. He is a Fellow of the Society of Antiquaries of London and a Member of the Chartered Institute for Archaeologists.

John Schofield was, until recently, Head of the Department of Archaeology at the University of York, where he is also Director of Studies in Cultural Heritage Management, having previously worked for English Heritage. John is a Fellow of the Society of Antiquaries of London, a Member of the Chartered Institute for Archaeologists and a Docent in Cultural Heritage, Landscape and Contemporary Archaeology at the University of Turku (Finland). He is also Senior Research Fellow at Flinders University, Adelaide, and an Adjunct Professor at Griffith University, both in Australia. He has published extensively in the fields of cultural heritage, archaeology of the recent and contemporary pasts, and the archaeology of conflict. As a child, John lived in Berlin (1971–1973), where his father was Officer Commanding 26 Signals Unit, based both at RAF Gatow and at the Teufelsberg.

Through this detailed archaeological investigation of Teufelsberg, one of the most iconic sites of the Cold War, many of its well-kept secrets are revealed. The material remains bear witness not only to the facilities housing the cutting-edge technology of a past era, but also give a glimpse of the everyday life of the many men and women that served there. This innovative study clearly shows the potential of contemporary archaeology to uncover hitherto unknown aspects of the recent past and may serve as a blue-print for future studies of secret installations.

Professor Mats Burström, *Stockholm University*

An engagingly written and well-illustrated study of an iconic site of twentieth century conflict heritage, and a valuable contribution to the rich literature on the ruins, relics and remains of Berlin. It will be of interest and value to heritage professionals, scholars of espionage and the Cold War, and urban explorers and others fascinated by the material traces of the recent past.

Dr Gabriel Moshenska, *UCL Institute of Archaeology*

Visible from afar, the white radomes of the Teufelsberg have always marked the most intriguing Cold War site in Berlin. This book lifts the veil of secrecy that shrouded this installation for decades, takes the reader back in time to the direct confrontation between the West and the East that characterised Berlin, and discusses the many layers of cultural significance embodied in the place.

Professor Leo Schmidt, *Brandenburg University of Technology Cottbus*

Routledge Archaeologies of the Contemporary World
John Schofield
University of York

A historian once described 'all history as contemporary history'. All archaeology is contemporary for the same reason – in its persistence, its resilience, its place in the contemporary world, on or beneath its surface. But increasingly archaeologists are focusing attention on the contemporary world itself, its materiality, the behaviours that underlie it, and the heritage it creates. Archaeology provides a distinctive and meaningful contribution to understanding the contemporary world – a contribution grounded in materiality, and in seeking to understand the often complex relationships between people, their behaviours and things. This series of books will generate new and deeper explorations of these relationships, creating and promoting archaeologies of the contemporary world through a range of formats (single-authored works, edited collections, Research Focus outputs) encouraging diversity of approach towards new interdisciplinary encounters with our supposedly 'familiar past'.

Archaeology of the Teufelsberg
Exploring Western Electronic Intelligence Gathering in Cold War Berlin
Wayne D Cocroft and John Schofield

After Discourse
Things, Affects, Ethics
Mats Burstrøm, Caitlin DeSilvey, Bjørnar Olsen, Þóra Pétursdóttir

Archaeology of the Teufelsberg

Exploring Western Electronic
Intelligence Gathering in
Cold War Berlin

**Wayne D Cocroft and
John Schofield**

LONDON AND NEW YORK

First published 2019
by Routledge
2 Park Square, Milton Park, Abingdon, Oxon OX14 4RN

and by Routledge
52 Vanderbilt Avenue, New York, NY 10017

First issued in paperback 2020

Routledge is an imprint of the Taylor & Francis Group, an informa business

British Library Cataloguing-in-Publication Data
A catalogue record for this book is available from the British Library

Library of Congress Cataloging-in-Publication Data
Names: Cocroft, Wayne, author. | Schofield, John, 1948– author.
Title: Archaeology of the Teufelsberg : exploring Western electronic intelligence
  gathering in Cold War Berlin / Wayne D. Cocroft and John Schofield.
Description: Abingdon, Oxon ; New York, NY : Routledge, 2019. | Series:
  Routledge archaeologies of the contemporary world | Includes bibliographical
  references and index.
Identifiers: LCCN 2018054365 | ISBN 9781138337107 (hardback) |
  ISBN 9780429442629 (ebook) | ISBN 9780429809620 (mobipocket
  unencrypted) | ISBN 9780429809637 (epub3)
Subjects: LCSH: Teufelsberg (Berlin, Germany) | Espionage, British—
  Germany—Berlin—History—20th century. | Espionage, American—
  Germany—Berlin—History—20th century. | Electronic intelligence—
  Germany—Berlin—History—20th century. | Berlin (Germany)—
  History—1945–1990. | Cold War. | Military archaeology—Germany—
  Berlin. | Berlin (Germany)—Antiquities. | Berlin (Germany)—Buildings,
  structures, etc. | Radomes.
Classification: LCC DD900 .C63 2019 | DDC 327.120943/15509045—dc23
LC record available at https://lccn.loc.gov/2018054365

ISBN 13: 978-0-367-67184-6 (pbk)
ISBN 13: 978-1-138-33710-7 (hbk)

Typeset in Times New Roman
by Apex CoVantage, LLC

Contents

Figures

Abbreviations

ASA	United States Army Security Agency (US); see also USASA
ASTRAB	Antenne de Service Technique de Recherche Avancée de Berlin (Fr)
BRIXMIS	The British Commander-in-Chief's Mission to the Soviet Forces in Occupation of Germany (UK)
FMLM	French Military Liaison Mission in Potsdam (Fr)
GCHQ	Government Communications Headquarters (UK)
GCR	Radio-electronic Communications Group (Fr)
INSCOM	Intelligence and Security Command (US)
RAF	Royal Air Force (UK)
SDECE	Service de Documentation Extérieure et de Contre-Espionage (Fr)
SIS	Secret Intelligence Service (UK)
SOU	Special Operations Unit (US)
SOXMIS	Soviet Military Liaison Mission(s) in Western Germany (SU)
Stasi	Ministerium für Staatssicherheit (GDR)
SU	Signals Unit (UK)
TCA	Tempelhof Central Airport (US)
USAF	United States Air Force (US)
USAFSS	United States Air Force Security Service (US)
USASA	United States Army Security Agency (US); see also ASA
USMLM	United States Military Liaison Mission in Potsdam (US)

Acknowledgements

The authors would like to thank the Berlin Wall Documentation Centre for funding fieldwork in 2011, through the support of its director Professor Dr Axel Klausmeier, and for subsequently supporting this publication. A key part of our project was to create a photographic characterisation of the site, and for this we enlisted the artist and photographer Angus Boulton. Angus accompanied us for our week of fieldwork, and made several of the key images used in this publication. We are indebted to Angus for his expertise and diligence, his extraordinarily perceptive approach and for his good company. We are grateful to Doug Robb, formerly of the RAF Air Defence Radar Museum, Neatishead, for details of his service at RAF Gatow. Surgeon Commodore Peter Buxton and Lt Col Paul Marks of the Defence Medical Group, DMS Whittington, provided insight into security arrangements both at the Teufelsberg and amongst allied forces in Berlin more generally. David Haysom of the RAF Linguists Association has generously provided notes from the Association's newsletter and recollections from his time in Berlin (1962–1973). Paul Mors, who served with 26 Signals Unit in the early 1970s, also kindly commented on and improved the text. Professor Leo Schmidt, Brandenburg Technical University (Cottbus), located and – with Anja Merbach – translated Stasi surveillance files on 26 Signals Unit and other western intelligence stations in West Berlin.

A thesis for the Berlin Technical University on Field Station Berlin by Katharina Beckmann, David Derksen, Robert Haesecke-Diesing and Florian Leitner (published as Beckmann et al. 2013) was of great assistance, and we are grateful to the authors for providing digital copies of their floor plans, which form the basis of some of our characterisation diagrams and associated interpretation. Katelyn Williams' (2014) dissertation included some additional first-hand accounts which we have used to support our interpretations. We are obliged to the people who answered our enquiries about post-war radio equipment: Alf Fisher, RAF Signals Museum, Henlow and John Delaney and Stephen Woolford, Imperial War Museum, Duxford.

Dr Gundula Bavendamm and Bernd von Kostka of the Allied Museum helped with arranging access to the site and archive material held by the museum. We are also grateful to EMGE security for permitting and facilitating access to the site. Finally, a number of people gave information on the site's 'afterlife' (Chapter 5). They have asked to remain anonymous, but we are grateful to them for the additional information they have provided on another phase of the site's history that is effectively without documentation.

English version

The authors would like to thank our German colleagues who helped to bring the German version of this book to publication, *Der Teufelsberg in Berlin* (Cocroft and Schofield 2016). Professor Dr Axel Klausmeier, Director of the Berlin Wall Documentation Centre, who skilfully co-ordinated the book's translation and publication; at the Zentrum für Militärgeschichte und Sozialwissenschaften der Bundeswehr, Potsdam, Dr Arnim Lang translated the book into German. Dr Annette Wolf at the Berlin Wall Documentation Centre carefully copyedited the original manuscript.

Summary

During the Cold War, Field Station Berlin, staffed by British and American personnel high on the Teufelsberg, an artificial hill raised from wartime bombing debris, was one of the West's most important electronic listening and intelligence-gathering posts. West Berlin lay over 100mi behind the Iron Curtain surrounded by communist East Germany and at the centre of the densest concentration of Warsaw Pact forces anywhere – a vast armed camp threatening the security of the West. From the vantage point of the Teufelsberg, British and American personnel monitored the electronic communications from the surrounding military forces, emissions that betrayed their organisation, technical capabilities and state of readiness, as well as high-level political intelligence. From the early 1960s, its white radomes and the now demolished red and white antenna tower rising above the wooded hill also became one of the city's most prominent landmarks. Today, the Teufelsberg stands as a contemporary and spectacular ruin, representing a relic of a lost cyber space of the Cold War and espionage, providing a rare and probably unique opportunity to closely investigate a modern signals intelligence facility.

Previous studies of the Teufelsberg (eg Behling and Jüttemann 2011; Beckmann et al 2013), drew on archives of the Allied Museum Berlin, which predominantly reflects the experiences of American intelligence personnel in Berlin. Further information on their contribution is available through these books and on veterans' websites and social media outlets. The British intelligence services are far more reticent about releasing information on their past activities, a reluctance that applies equally to their work in Cold War Berlin. In preparing this book the authors have consulted the available files at the United Kingdom's National Archives, including documents specially declassified for this work. In total, however, few documents were available, and those that were gave very little away. Thus, detailed information on the Teufelsberg's technical capabilities and the policy decisions taken as a result of the intelligence gathered remains beyond the reach of this generation of historians. Still less is known about French intelligence-gathering activities and few accounts are available in English, with the notable exception of Faligot (2001). This book therefore takes a different approach. Building on previous studies of redundant Cold War installations (eg Cocroft and Thomas 2003), the authors take an *archaeological* approach to the site, and specifically of the British presence there. This archaeological approach is based on the interpretation of what remains on the ground some years after the site was decommissioned and comprehensively cleared, presumably by the security services. This 'field evidence' is set in the context both of what is already known from published work, and from the few archival sources that are available. This unique and important study of an iconic ruin and strategically vital facility presents a counterpoint to and extension of previously published works, and provides an entirely new perspective on the Cold War.

Russian

Во время Холодной войны Берлинская полевая станция (Field Station Berlin), состоящая из британского и американского персонала и расположенная высоко на Чёртовой горе (Teufelsberg) – искусственном холме из обломков бомбардировок военного времени – была одним из самых важных западных пунктов электронного прослушивания и сбора разведывательной информации. Западный Берлин находился в более, чем в 100 милях за Железным занавесом, окружённый коммунистической Восточной Германией, в центре высочайшей концентрации сил Варшавского Договора со всех сторон – вооружённого до зубов лагеря, угрожающего безопасности Запада. Используя преимущества расположения Чёртовой горы, британский и американский персонал мониторил информацию, исходящую от окружающих военных объектов, информацию, которая разоблачала их организацию, технические возможности, состояние готовности, а также высокий уровень политической разведки. С начала 60-х белые обтекатели антенн и демонтированные ныне красно-белые антенные вышки, которые возвышались над лесистым холмом, стали наиболее известными достопримечательностями города. Сегодня Чёртова гора (Teufelsberg) – современные и впечатляющие развалины, представляющие собой пример потерянного киберпространства электронных выбросов и шпионажа Холодной войны, а также редкая возможность исследования современных сигналов разведывательного оборудования.

Предыдущие исследования Чёртовой горы (Teufelsberg), например – Behling and Jüttemann (2011), Бекман и другие (2013), использовали архивы Берлинского музея союзников (Allied Museum Berlin), который главным образом отражает опыт американской разведки в Берлине. Дополнительная информация о её деятельности доступна через книги и на ветеранских веб-сайтах. Британские спецслужбы гораздо более сдержаны в предоставлении информации об их прошлой деятельности в Берлине во время Холодной войны. В подготовке этой книги авторы сверялись с досье, доступными в Национальном архиве Соединенного Королевства, в том числе с документами, специально рассекреченными для этой работы. Тем не менее, информация о технических возможностях Чёртовой горы (Teufelsberg) и политические решения, принятые в результате собранных разведданных, остаются вне досягаемости этого поколения историков. Еще меньше известно о сборе разведданных французской разведкой. Немногие отчёты доступны на английском языке, примечательное исключение составляет Фальгот (Faligot, 2001). Поэтому, книга 'За стеной' неминуемо и неизбежно являет собой археологическое исследование места и, в особенности,, британского присутствия там. В связи с этим, исследование представляет собой, по меньшей мере, контрапункт к ранее опубликованным работам и их продолжение.

German

Während des Kalten Krieges befand sich die mit britisch – und amerikanischem Personal ausgestattete Field Station Berlin hoch oben auf dem Teufelsberg, einem künstlichen Hügel, der sich durch Trümmerschutt von Bomben aus der Kriegszeit aufgetürmt hatte und einer der wichtigsten elektronischen Abhör- und Nachrichtenbeschaffungsanlagen des Westens war. Westberlin lag über 100 Meilen hinter dem Eisernen Vorhang, umgeben vom kommunistischen Ostdeutschland sowie umringt von Mitgliedstaaten des Warschauer Paktes – ein riesiges bewaffnetes Lager, das die Sicherheit des Westens bedrohte.

Von dem Aussichtspunkt des Teufelsberges überwachte die britische und amerikanische Belegschaft die elektronischen Signale der umliegenden Streitkräfte; dazu gehörten Aussendungen, die ihre Organisation verrieten, die Ausspähung von technischen Möglichkeiten und Bereitschaftszuständen sowie auch politische Informationsbeschaffung auf hohem Niveau. Seine weißen und inzwischen zerstörten roten Antennentürme, die über dem begrünten Hügel emporragten, galten seit den frühen 1960-er Jahren als eines der berühmtesten Wahrzeichen der Stadt.

Heute steht der Teufelsberg wie eine zeitgenössische und spektakuläre Ruine da, die ein Relikt aus einem verlorenen Cyberspace von elektronischen Absonderungen und Spionage eines Kalten Krieges darstellt und die seltene Gelegenheit bietet, eine modern Abhöranlage zu untersuchen. Früheren Untersuchungen des Teufelsberges, z.b. Behling und Jüttemann (2011) und Beckmann u.a. (2013), war es möglich, Archive des Alliierten Museums Berlin heranzuziehen, welches vorwiegend die Erfahrungen der amerikanischen Geheimdienstbelegschaft wiederspiegelt. Weitere Informationen über deren Tätigkeiten stehen mittels Bücher zur Verfügung sowie auf Websites von Veteranen.

Die britischen Geheimdienste sind viel vorsichtiger mit der Veröffentlichung über ihre vergangenen Aktivitäten; eine Zurückhaltung, die sich auch auf ihre Tätigkeit im Kalten Krieg in Berlin bezieht. Während der Vorbereitungen zu diesem Buch haben die Autoren die zugänglichen Akten aus dem Nationalarchiv des Vereinigten Königreiches herangezogen, inklusive solcher Dokumente, die speziell für diese Arbeit freigegeben wurden. Nichtsdestotrotz bleibt die Information über die technischen Einsatzmöglichkeiten des Teufelsbergs und die politischen Entscheidungen, die aus der Informationsbeschaffung resultierten, jenseits der Reichweite dieser Historikergeneration. Noch weniger ist über die Aktivitäten des französischen Geheimdienstes bekannt und wenige Berichte sind in englischer Sprache erhältlich mit der bemerkenswerten Ausnahme von Faligot (2001). Das Buch Über die Mauer ist deshalb unveryichtbar und zwangsläufig eine archäologische Untersuchung des Standortes, insbesondere der britischen Präsenz dort. In dieser Hinsicht stellt die Studie sowohl einen Kontrapunkt als auch eine Erweiterung von vorherigen Publikationen dar.

Während des Kalten Krieges befand sich die mit britisch– und amerikanischem Personal ausgestattete Field Station Berlin hoch oben auf dem Teufelsberg, einem künstlichen Hügel, der sich durch Trümmerschutt von Bomben aus der Kriegszeit aufgetürmt hatte und einer der wichtigsten elektronischen Abhör- und Nachrichtenbeschaffungsanlagen des Westens war. Westberlin lag über 100 Meilen hinter dem Eisernen Vorhang, umgeben vom kommunistischen Ostdeutschland sowie umringt von Mitgliedstaaten des Warschauer Paktes – ein riesiges bewaffnetes Lager, das die Sicherheit des Westens bedrohte.

Von dem Aussichtspunkt des Teufelsberges überwachte die britische und amerikanische Belegschaft die elektronischen Signale der umliegenden Streitkräfte; dazu gehörten Aussendungen, die ihre Organisation verrieten, die Ausspähung von technischen Möglichkeiten und Bereitschaftszuständen sowie auch politische Informationsbeschaffung auf hohem Niveau. Seine weißen und inzwischen zerstörten roten Antennentürme, die über dem begrünten Hügel emporragten, galten seit den frühen 1960-er Jahren als eines der berühmtesten Wahrzeichen der Stadt.

Heute steht der Teufelsberg wie eine zeitgenössische und spektakuläre Ruine da, die ein Relikt aus einem verlorenen Cyberspace von elektronischen Absonderungen und Spionage eines Kalten Krieges darstellt und die seltene Gelegenheit bietet, eine modern Abhöranlage zu untersuchen.

French

Durant la guerre froide, la station de renseignement de Berlin qui employait du personnel britannique et américain à Teufelsberg, une colline artificielle constituée de débris de bombardement pendant la guerre, était l'une des plus importantes stations d'écoute électronique et de collecte de renseignements de l'Ouest. Berlin-Ouest se trouvait à plus de 100 miles derrière le rideau de fer, encerclée par l'Allemagne de l'Est communiste, et au centre de la plus forte concentration des forces du Pacte de Varsovie, une vaste oalition armée menaçant la sécurité de l'Occident. Depuis le poste d'observation de Teufelsberg, le personnels britannique et américain a pu intercepter les émissions électroniques des forces militaires basées aux alentours, révélant ainsi l'organisation de leurs forces, leurs capacités techniques, leur état de préparation, ainsi que des renseignements politiques de haut niveau. Depuis le début des années 1960, ses radômes blancs et sa tour d'antenne rouge et blanche, aujourd'hui démolie, qui s'élevaient au-dessus de cette colline boisée sont devenus l'un des sites les plus emblématiques de la ville. Aujourd'hui, le Teufelsberg constitue une ruine contemporaine et spectaculaire, relique d'un cyber espace révolu, celui de l'espionnage des émissions électroniques durant la guerre froide, et une occasion rare d'étudier un centre de renseignement électromagnétique moderne.

Des études menées sur Teufelsberg, comme par exemple celles de Behling et Jüttemann (2011) et de Beckmann et al (2013), ont pu révéler, à partir des archives du Musée des Alliés à Berlin, l'expérience du personnel de renseignement américain à Berlin en particulier. De plus amples informations sur ces contributions sont disponibles dans plusieurs livres et sur des sites web d'anciens combattants. Les services de renseignement britanniques sont beaucoup plus réticents à divulguer des informations sur leurs activités passées: une réticence qui s'applique à leurs actions durant la Guerre froide à Berlin. En préparant ce livre, les auteurs ont consulté les fichiers disponibles aux Archives nationales du Royaume-Uni, y compris des documents spécialement déclassifiés à cette occasion. Néanmoins, les informations sur les capacités techniques de Teufelsberg et les décisions politiques prises à la suite des renseignements collectés demeurent cachées et hors de portée de cette génération d'historiens. Les activités françaises en matière de renseignements est un sujet moins connu. Peu de récits sont disponibles en anglais à l'exception notable de celui de Faligot (2001). 'De l'autre côté du Mur' constitue inéluctablement et inévitablement une enquête archéologique de ce lieu et traite en particulier de la présence britannique. Cette étude présente à cet égard un contrepoint et un prolongement des travaux publiés antérieurement.

Spanish

Durante la Guerra Fría, la estación de inteligencia de Berlín cuyo personal británico y estadounidense trabajaba en Teufelsberg, una colina artificial hecha con escombros de bombardeos durante la guerra, fue una de las estaciones de escuchas electrónicas y de recopilación de información más importantes del Oeste. Berlín Oeste se encontraba a más de 100 millas detrás de la Cortina de Hierro, rodeada por Alemania Oriental cuyo régimen era comunista y al centro de la mayor concentración de fuerzas del Pacto de Varsovia, una amplia coalición que amenazaba la seguridad del Occidente. Desde la estación de observación Teufelsberg, el personal británico y estadounidense pudieron interceptar las emisiones electrónicas de las fuerzas militares instaladas alrededor, revelando así la organización de estas fuerzas, su capacidad técnica y su buena disposición así como información política de alto nivel. Desde principios de la década de 1960, sus cúpulas blancas y la torre de antena color rojo y blanco, ahora demolida, que se elevaban por encima de la colina boscosa se convirtieron en uno de los monumentos más emblemáticos de la ciudad. Hoy en día, el Teufelsberg es una ruina contemporánea y espectacular, una reliquia de un espacio cibernético pasado, el del espionaje de las emisiones electrónicas durante la Guerra Fría, y una rara oportunidad de estudiar un centro de inteligencia electromagnética moderno.

Estudios sobre Teufelsberg, tales como los de Behling y Jüttemann (2011) y Beckmann (2013) han puesto de manifiesto a partir de los archivos del Museo de los Aliados en Berlín, la experiencia del personal de inteligencia estadounidense en Berlín. Información acerca de esas contribuciones están disponibles en varios libros y en los sitios web de veteranos. Los servicios de inteligencia británicos son mucho mas reticentes a comunicar información sobre sus actividades pasadas: una reticencia que se aplica a sus acciones durante la Guerra Fría en Berlín. Durante la preparación de este libro, los autores consultaron los datos disponibles en los Archivos Nacionales del Reino Unido, incluyendo los documentos que han sido desclasificados especialmente para esta ocasión. Sin embargo, la información sobre la capacidad técnica de Teufelsberg y las decisiones políticas tomadas como resultado de la información recolectada, permanecen ocultas, fuera del alcance de esta generación de historiadores. Son au'n menos conocidas las actividades de recopilación de información de los franceses. Pocos testimonios estan disponibles en inglés, con la notable excepción de Faligot (2001). 'Al otro lado del Muro' lleva a cabo inevitable e ineludiblemente, un estudio arqueológico del sitio y trata en particular, de la presencia británica. En este sentido, el estudio presenta un contrapunto y una extensión a los trabajos publicados anteriormente.

1   Introduction: Berlin becomes the Cold War espionage capital

Berlin's history is long and complex. It is a city known for its troubled past, not least over the course of the twentieth century in which legacies of the Second World War and Cold War periods have become deeply ingrained in her character (eg Ladd 1997). Nowhere is this more keenly felt than at some of the city's key landmarks: the Jewish memorial and site of Hitler's bunker, close to the Brandenburg Gate, and at the Topography of Terror where Nazi and Cold War remnants are juxtaposed. But it is the city's Cold War legacies that are the subject of this book, legacies that present Berlin at the heart of European if not global Cold War history, and on the front line between East and West for much of the later twentieth century. After the end of the Second World War in May 1945, Berlin was divided into four occupation zones or 'sectors' controlled by the wartime allies: the United States, Great Britain, France and the Union of Soviet Socialist Republics. Throughout the ensuing Cold War (1946–1989), the city's strategic location between what had become East and West ensured that Berlin became the prime location for western intelligence services. (Figure 1.1).

By the 1980s, the significance of West Berlin as an intelligence-gathering centre was such that huge numbers of personnel were engaged in this activity. For example, of the 5,000 United States American military and civilian personnel in the city, 40 percent were employed in intelligence or counter-intelligence activities, additional to British and French personnel (Herrington 1999, 6). As well as military intelligence gathering carried out by the service teams, other allied security agencies, including the United States' Central Intelligence Agency (CIA) and the National Security Agency (NSA) and British staff from the Government Communications Headquarters (GCHQ) also operated from various listening stations in the city. More shadowy organisations, including the British Secret Intelligence Service (SIS), also exploited the special position of Berlin to mount operations against East Germany (Maddrell 2012, 48). The co-location of American and British intelligence personnel at sites including the Teufelsberg was one expression

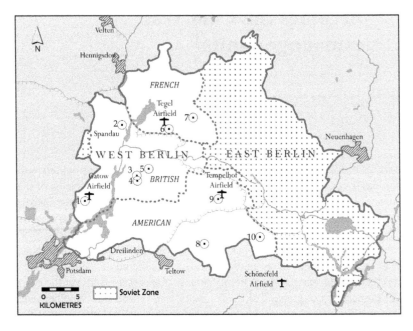

Figure 1.1 Cold War Berlin showing the occupation sectors and principal western signals intelligence-gathering sites

Source: Redrawn from Department of State 1961 *Background Berlin – 1961* Department of State: Washington DC, page 8

  1 Royal Air Force Gatow

  2 Spandau, Horchstelle, French Intelligence Services and later elements of the West German Bundesnachrichtendienst

Spandau – British Secret Intelligence Services, listening post

  3 The Teufelsberg, INSCOM Site 3, United States Army, RAF, British Army

  4 The Grunewald, INSCOM Site 4, United States Army, formerly Block 87

  5 Andrews Barracks, Finckensteinallee, Lichtertfelde, INSCOM Site 2 southeast of barracks, United States Army

  6 Tegel – French Army and Air Force, and later elements of the West German Bundesnach-richtendienst

  7 Cíte Foch, Rue Montesquieu, Reinickendorf – French Intelligence Services

Camp Napoléon, Reinickendorf – late 1940s French Intelligence Services

  8 Marienfelde, Didersdorfer Weg – United States Air Force

  9 Tempelhof Airport – United States Air Force

10 Rudow, Site 1 – CIA/United States Army

of the now widely known 'special relationship' between the two countries, cemented by a top secret pact on the sharing of intelligence signed in 1948 (Stafford 2002, 51).

Set within this wider context of complex geopolitics and regular episodes of tension, and given Berlin's strategic location on the Cold War's front line, this book explores the various ways in which surviving physical evidence creates opportunities for understanding a subject barely represented by available documentary and oral historical sources. This is because documents that relate to matters of continued relevance as matters of national security remain classified after the period of the '30 Year Rule' has elapsed. Equally, those who worked at the Teufelsberg signed the Official Secrets Act (an Act of Parliament that cannot later be 'unsigned'), and therefore commit an offence in speaking out, although this is more likely to be implemented in matters of strategic importance than in revealing the purpose of specific rooms within the complex. Given this lack of documentary information, and building on other archaeological studies of the contemporary past (eg Harrison and Schofield 2010) and the Cold War in particular (Cocroft and Thomas 2003; Schofield and Cocroft 2007), this study is presented specifically as an archaeological investigation of the buildings, as well as the often subtle traces within and around them, that modern military activities leave behind. Significantly, this is the first use of archaeological methods to investigate the undercover world of Cold War signals intelligence, and the first time a former intelligence-gathering site has been subjected to such close and critical scrutiny, a unique opportunity made possible only through its abandonment as an operational facility, but retention as a ruin. It is for this reason that the description of the facility is presented in close detail. In short, there may never be another opportunity.

In amongst the abandoned ruins of the Teufelsberg today, we should not forget that this was also a place of work for very large numbers of people, the identities of most of whom will never be known. There are however some notable exceptions. References exist within the text to Wing Commander A E Schofield, who was Officer Commanding 26 Signals Unit in Berlin from 1971–1973, a role that involved command of the British operations at the Teufelsberg. This was John's father. They lived on RAF Gatow during this time, and John recalls watching his father leave for work, in his black Opel with a flag on the bonnet, to his office at RAF Gatow, or on the Teufelsberg. While John was often shown the Teufelsberg as a distant landmark, from the opposite side of the River Havel, he never went closer, and his father never said anything to him or to his wife about what went on there. John's father died in 2001 and took his knowledge of the Teufelsberg with him. Conducting field-based research on any recent site or building which has a strong personal connection gives proximity that is unfamiliar for archaeologists who typically only encounter sites of earlier periods. Archaeologists are not trained for this close proximity, which can feel uncomfortable. There is also an argument that studies and assessment of the significance of such recent places can lack objectivity for this reason, although recent developments in understanding social value within a heritage context have created more systematic frameworks for such judgements to be made (eg English Heritage 2008). John has the photograph of his father shown in Figure 1.2 on his desk, a photograph his father always told him was taken at the Teufelsberg.

John naively hoped to find this office during the project, but given the condition of the site and the changes made since his father left in 1973, this was never likely to happen. To see his signature in Operational Records Books, however, partly made up for this disappointment, while the process of conducting the research also drew them closer. A short essay about John's time in Berlin and his connections with Gatow and the Teufelsberg has been previously published (Schofield and Schofield 2005).

The book begins (in Chapter 2) by summarising the geopolitical context and the presence of signals and intelligence in Berlin, amongst the British, American and French forces. Chapter 3 then considers in more depth the activities of British and American units at the Teufelsberg, before going

Figure 1.2 Wing Commander A E Schofield, Officer Commanding 26 Signals Unit 1971–1973, reputedly in his office at the Teufelsberg

Source: courtesy J Schofield

on (in Chapter 4) to describe the archaeological approach adopted for this investigation. Chapter 5 then contains a detailed site description, presenting the only such description available for a signals intelligence site of this Cold War period. This descriptive chapter is intended to serve as a record of the site's extant remains at the time of survey (Summer 2011), and as the basis for self-guided exploration. Chapter 6 then provides an architectural summary, before Chapter 7 explores the site's 'afterlife', prior to providing some general discussion and conclusions. We begin with the start of intelligence gathering in Cold War Berlin, immediately after the close of the Second World War.

2 Electronic intelligence gathering: beginnings

All military signals units are aware that their transmissions may be intercepted, and also of their capacity to eavesdrop on the transmissions of opposing forces. From the arrival of the western allied occupation forces in Berlin in July 1945, radio operators would have been conscious of their ability to pick up Soviet radio transmissions. That said, post-war reductions in military spending had led to a rapid run down in allied wartime intelligence capabilities, and there is no evidence of any systematic attempts to analyse Soviet radio traffic collected in Berlin during the late 1940s. Even during the intense air activity during the Berlin Airlift, 1948–1949, it does not appear that Soviet activity was routinely monitored. Yet contemporary British intelligence assessments had commented that the Soviet Army used mainly landlines and was comparatively poorly equipped with wireless equipment. It also warned British units of the Soviet army's skill in radio interception (War Office 1949, 54–55). The United States Army Security Agency (USASA) was equally poorly resourced and until at least 1949 was passing its material to the British Government Communications Headquarters (GCHQ) for analysis (Aldrich 2001, 77). From 1950 however the situation became increasingly complex, and for clarity we can divide Allied intelligence gathering in Berlin by the three allies present in the city: the British, the Americans and the French. It is also important to recognise the three main areas of activity:

SIGINT – *Signals intelligence*

Signals intelligence may be further subdivided into three areas:

COMINT – *Communications intelligence*, the interception, collection and analysis of radio, wire or other electronic communications.
ELINT – *Electronics intelligence*, the interception and analysis of electronic signal.

RADINT – *Radar intelligence*, the collection and analysis of data from foreign radar, telemetry stations and beacons, and also information gathered from the tracking of aircraft, missiles and other moving objects.

PHOTOINT – *Photographic intelligence*
HUMINT – *Human intelligence*, including information provided by spies and agents, and in this case by the official western military missions operating in East Germany.

The British

British intelligence-gathering activity in Cold War Berlin was initially focussed at RAF Gatow, the British occupation force's airfield, a former Luftwaffe training base located at the western extremity of the British occupation zone, with part of its boundary set against the sector boundary with the East. The station also acted as the parent unit for the successive signals intelligence units, covering many of their functional requirements, including accommodation. The station's Operational Record Books provide some information on the signals units' facilities. Elsewhere in the city British personnel also worked alongside the Americans at Rudow, Marienfelde and at the Teufelsberg.

From at least 1947, the RAF commenced a programme of 'ferret' flights along the Iron Curtain by modified Lancaster and Lincoln aircraft principally to gather information on the capabilities of Warsaw Pact air forces (Aldrich 2001, 81). Across the British post-war occupation zone it also maintained a network of signals intelligence stations. The RAF's signals intelligence presence probably began with the Air Scientific Research Unit (ASRU), which was the precursor of 646 Signals Unit formed on 1 September 1952. The unit controlled all the high frequency/direction finding and intercept teams in West Germany (Taylor 2003, 223). Some of the main radio interception stations were in north Germany at RAF Uetersen, Schleswig-Holstein, and to the south at Hambühen, Lower Saxony, 7 km west of Celle. In 1954 its staff of 220 operated 18 monitoring posts, many of which were mobile units that travelled along the West German border in search of places to intercept transmissions from the east (Elliot and Shukman 2002, 175). Another important listening post was established at the high vantage point of Schloss Scharfoldendorf, Lower Saxony. In 1957, Uetersen was closed and most of its personnel were moved to RAF Butzweilerhof, Cologne (Jackson 2001, 40, 57). Other significant RAF intercept stations were located at Dannenberg, Degerndorf and Wesendorf (Aldrich 2010, map). British occupation forces arrived in Berlin during July 1945, and with them came signals units to support the occupying forces' missions (Figure 2.1).

As the Cold War divisions hardened, Berlin's position at the heart of East Germany proved ideal for intercepting Warsaw Pact communications. The origins of co-ordinated intelligence-gathering operations in Berlin are obscure. From about 1951, a small permanent station was set up with three or four people on the top floor of Lancaster House, Fehrbelliner Platz (Figures 2.2 and 2.3).

Figure 2.1 British Berlin occupation forces arm badge

Source: W D Cocroft

Figure 2.2 Rathaus Wilmersdorf, Fehrbelliner Platz. In the early 1950s it was known as Lancaster House. The British used a section of its top floor for intercepting Soviet radio communications

Source: W D Cocroft

Figure 2.3 Rathaus Wilmersdorf, Fehrbelliner Platz. British-style letterbox on the front of the building

Source: W D Cocroft

This was perhaps the Assistant Director of Intelligence's Berlin listening station referred to in a letter enquiring if it could be used to intercept signals from the newly introduced Russian Ilyushin IL-28 jet bomber based at Oranienburg air base (Jackson and Haysom 2014, 104–105). From 29 March 1951, a small group of linguists and wireless operators, designated No.3 Detachment of 365 Signals Unit, from RAF Uetersen, was established at Gatow, working initially in two rooms on the upper floor of the headquarters and air traffic control building (Block 24) (Jackson and Haysom 2014, 104–105) (Figure 2.4).

Figure 2.4 RAF Gatow, headquarters and air traffic control building. During the early 1950s, British linguists used the upper floor of this building to listen into Warsaw Pact transmissions

Source: W D Cocroft

They were later attached to 646 Signals Unit and were responsible for collecting electronic intelligence (ww2.warwick.ac.uk/fac/soc/pals/staff/alrich/vigilant/lectures/gchq/646_su_memories_2.doc). In 1952, an RAF Regiment guard was stationed on the staircase to control access (Haysom pers. comm.). Probably soon afterwards the detachment from 646 Signals Unit established itself in a wooden hut on the roof of the air traffic control building.

By 1955, concerns were being raised that if another major crisis arose in Berlin, such as another Soviet blockade of the land routes into the city, then more accommodation might be required in the headquarters building, with the work of linguists in most demand. In September 1955 it was decided, therefore, to move this operation to the Hanbury Block, Block 15, a well-built 1930s former Luftwaffe building on the corner of Trenchard Road and Halton Road, which was then at the eastern perimeter of the airfield. It was probably named after Lady Felicity Hanbury, the first director of the Women's Royal Air Force (WRAF) (Jackson and Haysom 2014, 156–157: Haysom pers. comm.). Unfortunately, the Operational Record Book for RAF Gatow doesn't survive for this period. Throughout 1956 a later volume notes that conversion work for signals use was underway on Block 15, including the installation of air conditioning and signals fittings for the 'penthouse'. In December 1956, two floors were handed over to the signals detachment (TNA: AIR 28/1362 January 1956, December 1956; TNA: 28/1584 map) while the following year saw a small Stand-by Set (generator) House and an 115ft (35m) wooden tower completed and approval given to seek tenders for a radome (TNA: AIR 28/1584 March 1957; July 1957). Immediately to the west of Block 15 the map in TNA: 28/1584 shows a small building, 318, which may represent the Stand-by Set House and emergency generator, while to its north three spots marked 46 A, B and C may be aerials or masts (TNA: AIR 28/1584 map). Equipment used by the RAF section included two Telefunken control consoles and standard Grundig tape recorders. The electronic intelligence surveillance team also moved over to Block 15 at this time, and again were accommodated in a wooden hut on the roof (Haysom pers. comm.). For the remainder of the decade and into the early 1960s the upper floor of the Hanbury Block was the centre of intelligence-gathering operations, with the RAF unit located on one side of the corridor and an army unit opposite (Figure 2.5).

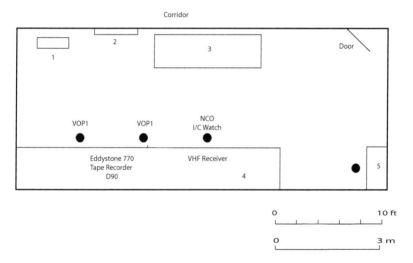

Figure 2.5 RAF Gatow, Hanbury Block, Army Set Room 1960

Source: www.langeleben.co.uk/Brian%20Patchett/brian_patchett_page1.htm, accessed 7 January 2016

1 'The Beast' – large upright reel-to-reel tape recorder

2 Map of East Germany and Soviet unit locations

3 Desk for non-commissioned officer in charge of the watch. He might also work at desk 4.

4 Desk for two voice operators listening to an Eddystone 770 Receiver. Each was provided their own tape recorder, but shared a D90 for reading scrambled voice and teleprinter traffic.

5 Administrative desk

At this time the RAF unit personnel worked a shift system of eight hours on and eight hours off for two or three days, and then two days off. Much of the information gathered was fairly routine. The often formulaic conversations between Russian pilots and their controllers nevertheless contributed to an understanding of the deployment and capabilities of opposing forces (Elliot and Shukman 2002, 184). Leslie Woodhead, a late 1950s national service Russian linguist, recalls the monotony of logging the call signs, fuel states and flying routines of the Russian pilots. The object was to detect any departure from ordinary routines. The working pattern for linguists revolved around 'long days', 5am to 12.30, and then 5pm to midnight, and 'short days', which lasted from 12.30 to 5pm, then a day off. The most unpopular shift was 'mids', from midnight to 8am (Woodhead 2005, 110). By the late 1950s the operation comprised five RAF officers, 152 other ranks, and 40 Royal Signals personnel (TNA: AIR 28/1362 May 1959). Interception work continued in Hanbury Block until about 1963, after which date it was converted to a recreation centre. During Group Captain Jack Wilson's tenure as station commander (1971–1974) the facilities were improved and it subsequently became known as 'Wilson's Retreat' (pers. comm. P Mors).

To support the unit's activities a remote Direction Finding Tower, about 3m tall, was sited close to the airfield's western perimeter and the sector boundary with East Berlin. Its function was to detect the movement of Warsaw Pact aircraft. One operator claimed it failed to work correctly, but survived in operation until about 1970 (Woodhead 2005, 111–114; Haysom pers. comm.). At the extreme western end of the airfield were two Circularly Disposed Antenna Arrays, one 97m in diameter and the other 180m in diameter; these may have been used for locating the position of radio signals or navigation aids (www.google.co.uk/intl/en_uk/earth/).

During the 1950s, and until the end of National Service in 1962, the British government's policy was to train a pool of conscripts that could then be drawn upon in any future conflict. This involved a 12 month training course, followed by six months practical training with a unit, and about six months of productive work. After the end of conscription, airmen with an aptitude for languages were recruited. To all appearances, RAF Gatow might seem like an attractive posting with access to Berlin and excellent sports facilities. But, the change in the demography of the unit, and the wider air force, brought new challenges and resentments. For example, a lack of married accommodation on the base was not resolved until the 1970s. As within any large organisation, tensions existed between different groups. In the case of the linguists, this division was aggravated by the signals units' irregular shift pattern, which was used, with the secrecy surrounding their work, as an excuse to evade routine station duties, exercises and parades. To the other station personnel they were known as the 'fairies' (Haysom pers. comm.). In the early 1960s a report on the defection of an army corporal suggested that tensions between the army and the RAF were exacerbated by the personality of a particular commander of the Royal Signals detachment. Differing shift patterns between the two units also created further dissatisfaction (TNA: WO32/20353, pieces 8 & 11).

In the 1950s, summaries information from Gatow was provided daily by teleprinter to its parent unit and GCHQ. These included 'spot' summaries of intercepts that might point to a new development or relate to an urgent operational need. Daily technical summaries were also provided with details of the traffic logged, radio frequencies and their call signs. This was followed by an initial intelligence assessment of the material. Hard copies of transcripts and the original tapes were sent daily under armed guard to the British Security Intelligence Service MI6 and the US Army Security Agency Unit based at Tempelhof Airport (Elliot and Shukman 2002, 187). The tapes rarely left the city, although transcripts might be sent out of Berlin on the daily British military train 'The Berliner', or given to the pilot of a British commercial airliner. Most of the detailed analysis of data intercepted in Berlin was analysed in the United Kingdom or the United States. However, the analysts based in Berlin provided instant warning of any unusual movements by Warsaw Pact forces.

RAF 26 Signals Unit

From 1962 intercept activities at RAF Gatow were concentrated in Hangar 4, one of eight hangars on the airfield, and another former Luftwaffe building (Taylor 2003, 223). At this date the Russian, Czech and German linguists moved to the hangar. To the station's personnel it was known simply as 'The Hangar', where initially it specialised in the interception of voice communications and electronics intelligence.

In the mid-1960s there was a major reorganisation of the British intercept stations. In 1966, partly to accommodate the arrival of No.5 Signals Wing headquarters, Hangar 4 underwent a major refurbishment programme. By September 1966, the transfer was almost complete and, coinciding with the move, No.5 Signals Wing was renamed 26 Signals Unit and for the remainder of the Cold War was synonymous with Royal Air Force signals intelligence work in Berlin (Figure 2.6).

In the following year Schloss Scharfoldendorf was closed and also RAF Butzweilerhof, Cologne, the former headquarters of No.5 Signals Wing. Brief accounts of the monthly activities of all RAF units are maintained in Operational Record Books, which after a period of time are released to the United Kingdom's National Archives at Kew. To date four such books for 26 Signals Unit, covering the period September 1966 to December 1982,

Figure 2.6 26 Signals Unit badge, Immer Wachsam – Always Alert. The inscription reads 'Presented to Wg Cdr A E Schofield by the officers of 26 SU July 1973'

Source: courtesy J Schofield

have been released (TNA: AIR 29/3881; TNA: AIR 29/4332, TNA: AIR 29/4578 and TNA: AIR 29/4927); at least two others remain retained by the government. They follow a standard pattern with brief notes on operational, administrative and engineering matters. Various returns record visits by other units and organisations that had an interest in their work, including the US Army Security Agency, United States Air Force, British Army of the Rhine, the Ministry of Defence, and redacted names whose affiliation may only be guessed at. They may also be used to outline some of the building campaigns at RAF Gatow and the Teufelsberg, and to identify some of the equipment in use. They do not, however, contain information on the surveillance operations mounted from these sites, nor transcripts of intercepted information. Records confirm that, in 1967, the unit's strength was about 350, rising to nearly 370 by 1973, but fluctuated from month to month as personnel were posted in and out (TNA: AIR 29/3381 and TNA: AIR 29/4332).

Hangar 4 RAF Gatow

As described above, the interception facilities were moved into a former Luftwaffe hangar which survives within the Luftwaffe's General Steinhoff barracks and is visible from the Luftwaffe Museum. Today, adjacent to the hangar, are two tall towers surmounted by radomes. These date from at least the mid 1960s. The shorter one was known as Alpha Tower and the taller one Blue Canyon Tower; a third tower, the Pirelli Tower, located adjacent to the fire station, has been demolished (Figure 2.7).

Intercept personnel moved into the hangar in the early 1960s and early in 1966, in anticipation of its expanded role, a refurbishment programme was put in place. By April, work was underway on the Pirelli Tower and

Figure 2.7 RAF Gatow: from the mid 1960s until 1990 Hangar 4 was the centre of RAF intelligence-gathering activities. The shorter tower was known as the Alpha Tower and the taller one Blue Canyon Tower; a third tower has been demolished

Source: W D Cocroft

improvements to the hangar's interior continued until early 1967. A new generator was also installed and steady progress was reported on special signals facilities (TNA: AIR 28/2014 Apr 66; Jul 66; June 67; TNA: AIR 29/3881 January 1967). Beneath the towers' domes were rotating antennae designed to intercept different radio frequencies. Some radio-location and monitoring was manufactured by the Munich-based Rohde and Schwarz electronics company (TNA: AIR 29/3881, October 1967). The Pirelli Tower was the responsibility of 646 Signals Unit, who had also moved their operations to Hangar 4, and was used for gathering signals intelligence (Haysom pers. comm.).

Equipment inside the hangar included voice recording equipment, while in 1968 a large consignment of British-manufactured Ferrograph Series 7 reel-to-reel tape recorders was delivered and 72 were available for use by the following March (TNA: AIR 29/3881, December 1968, March 1969). This communications centre had secure links to other intercept stations at the Teufelsberg and Marienfelde (TNA: AIR 29/3881, November 1969). In the late 1960s, Dave Haysom (pers. comm.) recalls that personnel worked in the offices surrounding the main hangar space. Shortly after Hangar 4 was occupied, between two and four brick offices were built in the hangar for traffic analysts. The activities within Hangar 4 were of great interest to the East Germans and Soviets, and on the opposite side of the border they built a watchtower to monitor activity. To counter this, a protective or screening wall was built to conceal the entrance and to prevent the observation of personnel movements. Here we see the Cold War in microcosm – a building being constructed, a surveillance tower to watch over it, and counter-surveillance measures being introduced to prevent this, all in the architecture of a German airfield.

A graphic illustration of the contemporary tensions in the city, and RAF Gatow's position on the Cold War front line, occurred during a meeting of the West German Bundestag held in April 1965. On 7 April, the Bundestag held a session in the Kongresshalle, Berlin, contrary to the understanding that West Germany should not involve itself in the affairs of West Berlin. To demonstrate their displeasure, for three days prior to the meeting Soviet jets were flown over the western part of the city, creating sonic booms. They also mounted low-level flights along the runways at Tegel and Templehof. On 6 April they carried out similar flights over Gatow, when the Soviet ground controllers on the opposite side of the border could be heard urging the pilots to fly even lower. In response, allied aircraft were taxied on the runways to prevent any landing attempts (Haysom pers. comm.).

Exactly a year later personnel from Gatow were involved in one of the most audacious intelligence missions of the Cold War. Radio operators became aware that a newly introduced Soviet Yakovlev Yak-28P (NATO codename Firebar) interceptor was in trouble over Berlin and that Soviet air traffic controllers were desperately trying to direct it for a crash landing on the East German side of the border (Figures 2.8 and 2.9).

Figure 2.8 April 1966, remains of the Soviet Yak-28 Firebar being lifted from the Stoessensee onto a barge for transfer to the Soviets. To the right is a British army crane. The uniformed personnel are mainly British, but also include West Berlin police and French and American personnel

Source: private collection

Figure 2.9 April 1966, remains of the Yak-28 Firebar's tail unit being lifted from the Stoessensee overseen by RAF police and West Berlin water police

Source: private collection

Unfortunately for the Soviets it fell short and crashed into a tributary of the Havel, the Stoessensee, about 2km northwest of the Teufelsberg and firmly in the British sector. With some danger from the live ejector seats, the bodies of the two-man crew, Captain Boris Vladislavovich Kapustin and First Lieutenant Yuri Nikolaevich Yanov, were extracted and handed back to the Soviets. Over the next few days and under the noses of a Russian shore party, but unknown to them, the British succeeded in removing the aircraft's state-of-the art Skip Spin radar and spiriting away its engines to the United Kingdom for analysis before returning them to the Russians (TNA: AIR 28/2014, 5–6; TNA: DEFE 44/473; Geraghty 1997, 133–142; Smith 2003; Kellerhoff and von Kostka 2012, 109–113).

From about 1975, Hangar 4 underwent a major refurbishment, starting with improvements to its security (TNA: AIR 28/2016 November 1975; December 1975). In July 1976, it was reported that work had started on a new signals tower for Hangar 4 (TNA: AIR 28/2215, July 1976). A year later, new computer equipment, air conditioning and additional security features were being installed (TNA: AIR 28/2215 August 1977; October 1977). In 1979, proposals were put forward for a new dish aerial and receiver site, and by October a new incinerator had been installed (TNA: AIR 28/2215, June 1979; October 1979). Security was further improved in 1980 when adjacent scrub was cleared to allow a barbed-wire fence to be laid (TNA: AIR 28/2215, April 1980). Work on the new dish aerial and receiver site were complete by November 1980 (TNA: AIR 28/2215, November 1980).

Radar intelligence

In 1983, a major advance in the RAF's intelligence-gathering capability occurred with the replacement of the obsolete air traffic control radar at Gatow with a Plessey Type 94 AR3D radar. This new three-dimensional radar mounted on top of a 60ft (18m) tower was outwardly to provide a new air traffic radar for Gatow, but also fed data into the joint Berlin Air Control Centre, with representatives from all four occupation powers.

To support its covert role a data-feed cable was also run into Hanger 4, where a small team of 23 people was able to monitor Warsaw Pact airspace across East Germany. This team was accommodated in three ISO (standard steel shipping) containers, placed in the hangar. The Operations Cabin sat on a raised concrete plinth, and was modified with a Faraday cage to prevent the interception of any electronic emissions. It was entered through doors with an airlock. Internally, it was divided into a number of compartments, including the operations area with four consoles across the width, the computer area with a number of output devices and large tables for laying out the very large printouts for study. In another area known as the Bureau, were terminals for the control of the powerful American supplied Digital Equipment Corporation (DEC) VAX computer and the production of reports. A clean room in the container housed this computer along with its Winchester hard disc drives and storage cupboards.

Almost abutting the Operations Cabin at one of its narrow ends was the administration area, comprising a further two ISO containers. One held the Administration Office, the Flight Sergeant's office and an office for the Squadron Leader in charge of the unit. Opposite this was another container with a very small office to provide quiet space for interviews, a storeroom and an all-ranks crew room for making drinks.

Prior to the initial deployment only a handful of senior non-commissioned officers had been 'indoctrinated' with the unit's tasks. To train the other operators the radar unit also borrowed rooms from 26 Signals Unit. The value of the information being produced was quickly recognised and a small team comprising a flight lieutenant and two sergeants, 'The A Team', was formed to provide more in-depth analysis of the data. In January 1984, another container was placed on top of the Operations Cabin for their use, and included a video-editing suite, briefing room, office for the flight lieutenant and an area for the sergeants.

The use of the radar for intelligence gathering marked a significant innovation and by coupling of the new radar to a VAX computer all of the collected data was able to be stored for later evaluation. Prior to this date the western allies were able to monitor Warsaw Pact air activity from the inner German border, although aircraft were only visible once they had climbed to a given altitude. The installation of this more sophisticated radar at the heart of one of the most militarised landscapes in the world gave the RAF unique capacity to monitor eastern aircraft movements. From this forward vantage point experienced fighter controllers were able to observe complete mission profiles from take-off to landing.

During its commissioning phase in 1983, the value of the system was quickly proved to the Americans. At this time, United States SR71 Blackbird spy aircraft sorties from RAF Mildenhall, Suffolk, into eastern Europe and the Soviet Union usually followed a standard route across Denmark and then eastwards. To evade interception they relied on speed and altitude. The new radar intelligence, however, revealed the potential vulnerability of this route and during one flight, a Soviet MIG 25 Foxbat fighter was detected being scrambled from Finow airfield, Eberswalde, to the north of Berlin. At one point it was observed to have missed an opportunity of launching its missiles by 3mi (4.8km), and furthermore had strayed into Danish airspace (Robb pers. comm.).

British army units

After 1945, the British army's signals intelligence work was principally the responsibility of Royal Corps of Signals, No.1 Special Wireless Regiment, which from the mid-1950s was based at Mercury Barracks, Birgelen, close to the Dutch border, where it remained until it was disbanded in 1995. In 1953, a detachment, known as 'Royal Signals Detachment Gatow', was established in Berlin, manned by Intelligence Corps Voice Ops, or linguists. On 1 September 1959, the Special Wireless Regiment was designated 13th Signal Regiment (Radio). The operational units also comprised elements from the Intelligence Corps and the Women's Royal Army Corps. It is not known where this unit was originally housed, but it too may have been based in the Gatow headquarters building, and the increase in numbers may have been another factor in moving to the Hanbury Block. Certainly by the late 1950s veterans describe being accommodated on the first floor of the Hanbury Block, on the opposite side of the corridor to the RAF detachment. The operational unit included two voice operators who were each equipped with the then new Eddystone 770 receivers for monitoring Mercury Grass communications, a tape recorder and access to the D90 for reading scrambled voice and teleprinter traffic. Mercury Grass was the codename for an American supplied radio that enabled the interception of high-level Soviet communications with Moscow. Also in the room was a large tape recorder, nicknamed 'The Beast', a British army type VHF receiver, and administrative desks. One veteran describes how, in 1960, the detachment numbered 23 people, comprising 12 'voice ops' (four non-commissioned officers and eight privates), and a commanding officer, who was also a Russian linguist. They were supported by a sergeant in charge of administration, two radio mechanics, four specialists for handling scrambled teleprinter messages, two of whom were assigned to the RAF for teleprinter cipher work, and a driver (www.langeleben.co.uk/Brian%20Patchett/brian_patchett_page1.htm). This is slightly fewer than in the official return of the previous year (TNA: AIR 28/1362 May 1959). Intercepted signals included the Soviet high frequency teleprinter and voice channel used by senior officers. Occasionally, certain weather conditions would also allow other more distant links to be monitored (Elliot and Shukman 2002, 185).

Security breaches were rare, but one of the worst occurred on 2 July 1963, when Corporal Brian Patchett of the Intelligence Corps defected to East Germany from his base at RAF Gatow (see box). Another damaging security leak also had its origins at Gatow, when Sergeant Geoffrey Prime offered his services to the Soviets (Aldrich 2010, 370–71). In 1968, after leaving the RAF, Prime began work at GCHQ and an espionage career that lasted until the early 1980s.

In 1967, the army detachment at Gatow was moved to the Teufelsberg, and three years later was renamed 3 Squadron, 13 Signal Regiment (Radio). It was finally disbanded in 1994 (www.birgelenvets.org/webpages/history.aspx).

Brian Patchett

One of the most notorious defections from the British occupation forces in Berlin was that of Corporal Brian Patchett (Figure 2.10).

At the age of 19, Patchett, from Coventry, had enrolled in the army's Intelligence Corps in July 1958 and in 1961 had gone on to pass the Russian Voice Interceptor Course, graduating as an Analyst Special Intelligence. Despite a known psychiatric history he was posted to join 13 Signals Regiment at Gatow in November 1962. The following spring he began a relationship with a temporary Navy, Army, Air Force Institute (NAAFI) German waitress, 21-year-old Rosemarie Zeiss, which she then ended. It appears that her termination of the friendship in June of that year was the catalyst for his defection. A contributing factor, however, was probably the poor working atmosphere at Gatow, with tensions between the commander of the army contingent and the RAF (TNA: WO32/20353, 5b). After writing a farewell note stating his intention to defect, he went over to East Berlin on 2 July 1963.

As a member of a signals intelligence unit, he was potentially a valuable catch for the East Germans and they delayed reporting his presence until 6 July. Although a junior rank, his previous postings had given him a good knowledge of United Kingdom and United

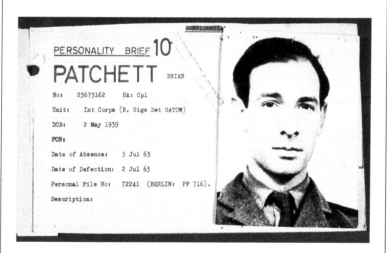

Figure 2.10 Corporal Brian Patchett. A 'mugshot' card maintained by BRIX-MIS of British defectors to the East

Source: TNA: WO208–5378

States interception techniques and capabilities. Extraordinarily, it was revealed that although Rosemarie was serving in a British services' canteen, her parents lived in Saalfeld, East Germany. The report into his defection concluded that it was a combination of his mental state, the poor working atmosphere at Gatow, and the ending of his relationship with Rosemarie Zeiss that had led him to defect. It also concluded that he had no known communist sympathies and it was thought unlikely that he had been turned by a foreign intelligence agency (TNA: WO32/20353, 4a).

Patchett's defection appears to have been for personal rather than political reasons and in particular unhappiness with his posting to Berlin. He, nevertheless, took with him a detailed knowledge of British and American signals intelligence in West Germany. How much Patchett compromised western intelligence gathering is unknown, as is his fate. It was rumoured that western defectors were moved to the eastern extremities of East Germany in the vicinity of Bautzen (TNA: WO32/20353), but beyond that nothing is known of his eventual whereabouts.

'Rocking Horse' – training for war

Exercises simulating the transition to a war footing were a regular part of Cold War service routines, sometimes carried out in full protective clothing, against nuclear, biological and chemical attack. In Berlin, surrounded by Warsaw Pact forces, regular 'Rocking Horse' exercises were held to practice the response to any attack on the city. During any period of building tension, Berlin's listening posts would provide an early warning of a Warsaw Pact attack and consequently would have been prime targets for sabotage or attack. Regular features of these exercises included practicing the denial and destruction of sensitive material. Signals personnel who rarely touched a weapon were also instructed in the use of various types of small arms (TNA: AIR 28/3881 October 1967; March 1970). In the 1960s, few personnel in 26 Signals Unit took the exercises seriously and many were notable by their absence (Haysom pers. comm.). The specialists who knew just how far western intelligence had penetrated Soviet systems were also at risk. In 1979, during a station defence exercise at Gatow, TRIAL CANTER, an operation codenamed LAMIA was put into place to evacuate key members of 26 Signals Unit (TNA: AIR 28/2215 June 1979). In the 1970s, in addition to threats from Warsaw Pact attack, units also improved their defences against terrorist attack from both West German terrorists and the Irish Republican Army. The Sailing Club associated with RAF Gatow was subject to bomb attack by a German terrorist group, the Movement 2 June, in February 1972 with the loss of one life (Durie 2012, 186).

The Americans

It was the outbreak of the Korean War (1950–1953) that caused the West to become increasingly concerned about Soviet intentions, and gathering information that might forewarn of an attack became a high priority. As a result, in 1951 the United States Army Security Agency (USASA), based in West Germany, moved a small tactical support unit from 6th Field Station Herzogenaurach, Bavaria ('Herzo Base') to Berlin (Figure 2.11).

Figure 2.11 United States Berlin occupation forces arm badge

Source: W D Cocroft

As one of the Cold War's potential flash points, throughout the 1950s more mobile units were posted to the city and on 1 January 1957, the army's unit was designated the 260th ASA Detachment with its headquarters at Andrews Barracks, Lichterfelde. In 1958, it was renamed the 280th ASA Company, with seven officers, two warrant officers and 136 enlisted personnel (Prock 1992). At first the army operated from mobile vans moving around the ruined city to find suitable locations for signals interception. But as the Cold War division became a feature of Berlin life, so too the signals intelligence units adopted permanent sites. At Rudow, in the southeast corner of the American zone, a radio station was established, later known as INSCOM Site 1. In the mid-1950s this was the site of one of the most notable joint American and British operations when a tunnel was dug to tap into Soviet telephone lines (Stafford 2002; Durie 2012, 94–98; Kellerhoff and von Kostka 2012, 60–89). A section of this tunnel was recovered in 1997 and is now on display in the Allied Museum (Stafford 2002, 185–186).

During the Cold War, access to Berlin by western aircraft was restricted to three prescribed 'air corridors', and aircraft straying from these routes might be 'buzzed' or shot at by Soviet fighters. Around 1960, to assist aircraft en route to Berlin, powerful electronic navigation and jamming-resistant radar landing aids were installed at Tempelhof Airport. It was soon found, however, that these interfered with the interception facilities already located there (Figure 2.12).

As well as operating from the airport, monitoring was also carried out from mobile vans and it was discovered that a rubble mound in the southwest of the American sector on Diedersdorfer Weg, Marienfelde (one of several around the city, comprising ex situ bomb debris from the Second World War), was a particularly suitable place for them (Figure 2.13).

Therefore, to replace Templehof, a more permanent facility was established here in June 1962 comprising two mobile trailers and a wooden hut, while in the following year the number of trailers was doubled and permanent structures built. The site was expanded in 1965 and became fully operational by June 1967. It was primarily a United States Air Force facility and was mainly staffed by personnel from the 6912th Security Squadron (Figure 2.14).

The main function of the station was monitoring Warsaw Pact air forces, but it also had the capability to break into the Soviet long distance tropospheric communications system to intercept radio and data transfers (Mackris 2008, 276–277). If war had broken out there were also elaborate plans to misdirect Soviet aircraft by breaking into their fighter communication systems (Mackris 2008, 99). The site of Marienfelde has subsequently been levelled, although the rubble mound of course remains.

Figure 2.12 Tempelhof was known to the United States forces as Tempelhof Central Airport, TCA or T-Hof. In the early 1950s signals intelligence units occupied the sixth floor of the eastern end of the airport building. The 72m radar tower was added during the 1980s and in addition to allied air traffic control functions it was probably also used to track Warsaw Pact air activity

Source: W D Cocroft

BStU-Kopie

Figure 2.13 Marienfelde, Didersdorfer Weg, United States listening station photographed by East German intelligence agents from the eastern side of the Berlin Wall

Source: BtSU MfS-HA-1–17659-Seite-0068: S.16 lower

Figure 2.14 Tempelhof painted glass window commemorating the United States
Air Force's 6912th Security Squadron that operated in Berlin from the
late 1950s

Source: W D Cocroft

Block 87 or INSCOM Site 4

About 1.5km to the south of the Teufelsberg is the site of INSCOM 4,
previously known as Block 87 after the forest unit in which it was situ-
ated. It comprised an antenna field and associated blockhouse, all surrounded by a chain link fence (Pellington nd). The site was cleared in the
1990s, but its large levelled platform, measuring 263m x 193m, and other
traces of the site's former use, remains. Historic air photography taken
in Berlin December 1953 (available through www.google.co.uk/intl/en_
uk/earth/) shows most of the southern portion of the woodland block as

being clear while a small group of buildings was already in place at its southeastern corner, comprising a rectangular building set perpendicular to the main track, with what appears to be a covered way leading to another smaller building. To its north was a small fenced enclosure with two small buildings and tracks leading off to the west. A photograph, probably taken during the 1960s, shows the site had been reduced to a large building near the gate and a smaller building to its rear.

The site was entered from Verbindungschausee and two large oak trees with white painted trunks mark its entrance (Figure 2.15). To the west a line of saplings indicates the position of the boundary fence. Internally, a low L-shaped earthwork topped with silver birch and lime trees and a scatter of small fragments of building materials indicate the site of a building (Figure 2.16).

To its north a group of overgrown rose bushes and a cherry tree surrounded by rose bushes mark the overgrown remnants of a small garden plot. To the west of this area was an array of telegraph poles with climbing irons set into concrete. Some of these remain standing while others have been felled (Figure 2.17).

The only other traces of the site include occasional pieces of electrical cable, drain covers and a manhole cover marked 'electric'. In

Figure 2.15 These white painted trees marked entry to the site from the woodland track of Verbindungschausee

Source: authors

Figure 2.16 Line of silver birch trees indicating the edge of the access track
Source: authors

Figure 2.17 Felled timber post from the antenna field
Source: authors

Figure 2.18 Concrete tethering block for securing a steel cable to a radio mast
Source: authors

the next woodland block to the east are two concrete blocks, 1m ×
1m, with traces of fittings and steel cabling typical of those used to
secure radio masts. (Figure 2.18).

   Although this site lay in the British sector, it appears that from the
1950s it was continuously occupied by the United States Army Security Agency. And in contrast to its present peaceful woodland setting,
this may once have been a noisy place: a veteran recalled that music
was constantly played over loudspeakers here to prevent eavesdrop-
ping (http://fsbvg.org).

The French

Far less is known about French signals intelligence and their interception
sites. The French secret intelligence service, the Service de Documentation
Extérieure et de Contre-Espionage (SDECE), was responsible for monitoring diplomatic communications. In 1945, soon after the arrival of French
occupation forces in Berlin, they established an interception station at Camp
Napoléon, Reinickendorf (Figure 2.19).

   All other signals intelligence and processing was undertaken by the Radio-
electronic Communications Group (GCR), although most of their work was
for the SDECE. Within their headquarters at Cité Foch in Reinickendorfer,

Figure 2.19 French Berlin occupation forces arm badge
Source: W D Cocroft

north Berlin, they maintained an interception station with the acronym
ASTRAB (Antenne de Service Technique de Recherche Avancée de Berlin). In the early 1950s the French army's 42nd Régiment de Transmissions
and the French Air Forces Groupe Electronique 30.450 also established an
interception station at Tegel airport. Escadrons électroniques au sol (EES
02) operated the station during its final phase (Faligot 2001, 184–185, 199).
It has also been suggested that the French operated a radio interception site
at Horchstelle, Spandau (Schmidt-Eenboom 2001, 148).

The Cité Foch listening station was on the north side of the Rue Montesquieu in a compound 100m x 58m (Figure 2.20).

In its final phase it was surrounded by a post and horizontal slab fence
about 2m in height. This was topped with barbed wire and, to prevent objects
being thrown over the wall, its height was increased with an additional wire

Figure 2.20 Rue Montesquieu, Cité Foch, Reinickendorfer, French listening station
Source: W D Cocroft

mesh screen. Lighting and close-circuit television provided further security. The enclosure was entered through a single entrance on Rue Montesquieu, a sliding-steel gate for vehicles and a single door for pedestrians (Figure 2.21).

The main building, which was constructed sometime after 1953, is a large, rectangular, two-storey structure with a pitched tiled roof and dormer windows. There is also a small single-storey building set perpendicular to the road. Dominating the site was a huge red and white tower in the northwest corner of the compound. Subsequent to the withdrawal of the French forces in the early 1990s, the West German federal intelligence service, the Bundesnachrichendienst (BND), occupied the site for about a decade. After their departure the large tower was demolished, sometime between 2000 and 2005.

The French maintained a close working relationship with the BND and from the late 1970s the BND worked at a site adjacent to the French station at Horchstelle Spandau, and operated the station at Tegel jointly with the French. At the latter site, and to hide their activities from the British and Americans, the West German unit adopted the name *Arbeitsgruppe für Vergleichsuntersuchungen* (Working Group for Comparative Research) (Schmidt-Eenboom 2001, 148). French efforts were, however, compromised by East German penetration of their service, which also enabled the East Germans to devise ways to protect their own communications as well as feeding misleading data to ASTRAB (Faligot 2001, 195).

Figure 2.21 Rue Montesquieu, Cité Foch, Reinickendorfer, entrance to the French
     listening station

Source: W D Cocroft

Liaison missions

As part of the immediate post-war settlements the four allied pow-
ers established rights for military liaison missions to operate across
Germany. On the western side were the British Commander-in-
Chief's Mission to the Soviet Forces in Occupation of Germany
(BRIXMIS) (Figure 2.22), the United States Military Liaison Mis-
sion (USMLM), the French Military Liaison Mission in Potsdam
(FMLM), and a reciprocal Soviet Military Liaison Mission (SOX-
MIS) was accredited to the three occupation powers in Western Ger-
many. (Figure 2.23).

From their initial liaison role they evolved into efficient intelligence-gathering organisations with unique access through the Iron
Curtain. The British had the largest team with 31 Soviet issued
passes, while the Americans and French had a total of 32. The British were therefore able to mount more missions and operate regular
three-person tours (Geraghty 1997, 10). Some tours would be carefully planned to combine signals intelligence with on-the-ground

BRITISH COMMANDER-IN-CHIEF'S MISSION
TO THE SOVIET FORCES IN GERMANY

Figure 2.22 British Commander-in-Chief's Mission to the Soviet Forces in Germany (BRIXMIS) unit logo

Source: private collection

SIGHTING PROCEDURE

1. Whenever you see a Soviet military vehicle, report by telephone as quickly as possible to 43 21 (see Page 1), giving as many of the following details as possible:
   a. Date and time of sighting.
   b. Type/make/colour of vehicle.
   c. Vehicle registration numbers and other markings.
   d. Number of occupants and dress.
   e. Location and direction of travel.
   f. Any other items of interest.

2. A guide to cyrilic letters is at Page 3. Report the number plate or other markings as:
   a. FIGURES ... AND ... AND ... AND ...
   b. CYRILLIC LETTERS NUMBER ... AND ...

3. For example on Page 1 the report would be:
   a. FIGURES ZERO ZERO DASH EIGHT FOUR
   b. CYRILLIC LETTERS NUMBER 20 AND 9

4. Your report will always be useful, even if for some reason you are not able to make it immediately following the sighting.

Page 2

GUIDE TO CYRILLIC LETTERS

A	1	Л	12	X	22
Б	2	M	13	Ц	23
В	3	Н	14	Ч	24
Г	4	O	15	Ш	25
Д	5	П	16	Щ	26
E	6	P	17	Э	27
Ж	7	C	18	Ю	28
3	8	T	19	Я	29
И	9	У	20		
K	11	Ф	21		

Page 3

PROCEDURE

1. Soviet flag tours are not permitted to enter barracks, airfields, depots or other military installations, and are to be prevented from doing so.

2. Soviet flag tours are not to be:
   a. Followed.
   b. Blocked in by other vehicles or molested in any way.
   c. Told to move on by unit guard rooms.

3. Photographs of Soviet flag tours may be taken if necessary, so as to identify Soviet soldiers engaged in illegal activities. Exposed films suitably labelled are to be sent to HQ Berlin (British Sector).

Page 4

BERLIN FORM 53
(Revised August '83)

SOVIET MILITARY VEHICLES

00-84 ун

THIS IS A TYPICAL SOVIET MILITARY VEHICLE NUMBER PLATE

If you see a Soviet military vehicle, contact as quickly as possible:
RMP Duty Room 43 21
(if using a Civil Phone dial 309 43 21)

Page 1

Figure 2.23 Card issued to British personnel in Berlin instructing them how to report SOXMIS vehicles in the vicinity of western military installations

Source: private collection

observations, allowing links to be made between monitored signals traffic and units on exercise, or tours might be directed towards 'promising targets' (Geraghty 1997, 204–205, Holbrook 2008, 196). The bi-annual Soviet troop rotation was also carefully monitored. Radar and signals intelligence was able to observe the arrival and departure of troop transport aircraft. On the ground in East Germany, BRIXMIS personnel were able to confirm when the most senior Soviet troops had left, providing solid evidence that units were not being reinforced as a prelude to a pre-emptive attack (Robb pers. comm.).

RAF Gatow took administrative responsibility for the RAF personnel attached to BRIXMIS and maintained two small Chipmunk aircraft, supposedly for training, but modified with small camera ports that were also used to monitor Russian and East German activity in the Berlin area (Marsden 1998, 178–193; Wright and Jefferies 2015). Both these aircraft survive. The Allied Museum preserves one and the other remains in service with the RAF's Battle of Britain Memorial Flight based at Coningsby, Lincolnshire. (Figure 2.24).

Figure 2.24 RAF Chipmunk WG 486, pictured in 1998 at RAF Leuchars in its plain grey Berlin paint scheme. This aircraft was formerly based at RAF Gatow and was used to photograph the border fortifications and Warsaw Pact forces around Berlin

Source: private collection

Given the relatively small pool of Russian linguists and Warsaw Pact intelligence experts it is perhaps not surprising that there was regular interchange of personnel between different agencies. On at least one occasion a BRIXMIS RAF touring officer was transferred to 26 Signals Unit, and in another case a flight lieutenant from RAF Gatow was posted to GCHQ (TNA: AIR 28/2215 November 1976; TNA: AIR 28/2016 January 1974). By the 1980s, a standing three-monthly European Tactical Analysis Conference (ETAC) was hosted by the National Security Agency European Tactical Analysis Team at the Teufelsberg. This brought together the American and British intelligence agencies in West Berlin, including mission personnel, to prepare situation reports and assessments of particular types of equipment. The resulting reports were highly classified and few if any of the personnel present saw the full picture. By the mid-1980s, the combination of BRIXMIS' very active touring programme and the newly available radar intelligence provided the British with a further valuable source of information to continue the United States' self-interest in maintaining intelligence co-operation between the two countries.

The watched watch the watchers

Berlin was of less value to the Warsaw Pact as a surveillance centre than to its western counterparts. While the Warsaw Pact might learn relatively little about NATO's capabilities and intentions by monitoring the forces in West Berlin, the West's surveillance of the East nonetheless provoked active counter-intelligence operations. These were led by the Soviet Union and East Germany, while additional Warsaw Pact intelligence agencies were active, for example, in trying to 'turn' personnel with close links to East European émigré communities.

As the East German foreign intelligence service of the Ministry for State Security, or Stasi, headed by Marcus Wolf, became aware of the activities on the Teufelsberg, it became a high priority to understand its capabilities (Wolf 1998, 294). Wolf considered people might be enticed to betray secrets for a myriad of reasons. In one of the notorious espionage cases associated with the Teufelsberg, the betrayal of its secrets was achieved through a straightforward financial transaction. During the 1970s, one of the Stasi's most important recruiters was a Turkish motor mechanic, Huseyin Yildirim, who was employed in one of the Andrews Barracks' motor pools. As the main accommodation barracks for the field station it gave him access to personnel and an insight into weaknesses that might be exploited (Wolf 1998, 293).

Yildirim's most significant recruit was Specialist James W Hall, one of around 1300 employees of the National Security Agency at the Teufelsberg. One of the East German's main concerns was to discover the types of information being intercepted. These were extensive and included telephone conversations amongst the party elite, the telephone and radio traffic of the East German air force, and the communications of the Stasi. It was only at a late stage that the East Germans also discovered daily radio traffic reporting that the state of internal and external policies to the Central Committee had been broken, providing an insight to the parlous state of East Germany's economy (Wolf 1998, 294). Hall left Berlin to attend training in the United States, from which he returned to be head of electronic warfare and signals intelligence operations for the United States' 5th Corps in Frankfurt. Through his treachery it was discovered that through the ELOKA electronic warfare system, operators at the Teufelsberg were regularly monitoring Warsaw Pact deployments. He also passed on many manuals and documents describing procedures and areas of interest to the West. Hall was finally arrested in 1988, subsequent investigations revealing that he had originally been recruited by the KGB and had been double-dealing secrets to the East Germans (Herrington 1999, 319). His trial revealed that between 1982 and 1985 he had received $300,000 from the East Germans. The cost to the Americans in compromised programmes was immeasurably greater (Wyden 1989, 114; Wolf 1998, 296; Herrington 1999, 309–340). Not all attempts at subverting personnel of the Field Station were so successful, and in 1985 after a short operation four Soviet agents were apprehended while attempting to buy secrets from an American sergeant (Herrington 1999, 15–25; 45–56).

Through another spy, United States Air Force Sergeant Jeffrey M Carney, Stasi cover name 'Kid', a linguist and communications specialist based at Marienfelde, the Stasi discovered other aspects of the West's capabilities (Eichner and Dobbert 1997, 223; Carney 2013, 82–85). These included the ability on the outbreak of war to pinpoint key Warsaw Pact installations and to break into air communications at the Soviet Eberswalde air base. In 1984, he was spirited to the East, but after the fall of the Wall was finally apprehended in 1991 (Wolf 1998, 297; Carney 2013, 590–592).

Beyond these headline cases the vast bureaucracy of the Stasi gathered detailed information on the western intelligence sites, units and personnel. Surviving documents from the Stasi's Hauptabteilung II, Spionageabwehr (counter-espionage) unit provide some insight into the level of their knowledge and daily routines of their western targets. In a report prepared in 1978, through the acquisition of a telephone list, they were able to confirm the location of a number of interception units. The report also provided information on the addresses, telephone numbers, family circumstances and specialist knowledge of 24 senior members of 26 Signals Unit, including four civilian employees (BStU MfS HAII 34747, 0022–0031). It also paid particular attention to the security features at the Teufelsberg, including its double fence and entry arrangements, which was by a United States or British military identity card. It also drew attention to the German tradesmen from West Berlin companies who were employed within the compound, as they were perhaps regarded as susceptible to subversion (BStU MfS HAII 34747, 0022–0031).

A later report on 26 Signals Unit, probably compiled in 1984, summarises what was known about the unit, including the presence of linguists and its links to GCHQ (Figure 2.25).

Hangar 4 at Gatow was of special interest. It was noted that in late 1983 security around the hangar had been increased, which we now know can probably be linked with the arrival of the radar intelligence unit. They also had a general idea of the contents of Hangar 4, including its computer, print shop, photography laboratory and other unknown technical equipment. Defences around this building were known to include a double fence with a 25m-wide clear strip and dog patrol, guard posts, lighting and electronic security measures. Entry into the hangar was via coded red cards and inner locking doors (BStU MfS HAII 34747, 0256–0258). They further estimated that about 55 British personnel and ten officers worked at the Teufelsberg.

BStU-Kopie

Figure 2.25 This group photograph of intelligence personnel from the Teufelsberg was discovered in Stasi (Ministerium für Staatssicherheit) archives

Source: BtSU MfS-HA-11–34747-Seite-0031

The report also discussed the military bus that took the British personnel between Gatow and the Teufelsberg for their shifts. Perhaps this was perceived as a vulnerable link in the system (BStU MfS HAII 34747, 0257).

From context to the site itself

Having now presented an overview of the political and social contexts in which to view the activities conducted at the Teufelsberg, and their significance, we can now turn to the site itself. At the time of writing, the Teufelsberg remains a prominent landmark within the western suburbs of Berlin, but one only officially accessible by guided tour. Many visitors do access the site illegally. The site is as complex as it is dangerous. Parts of the site are in complete darkness, and hidden dangers exist in the form of holes in the floor, broken glass and some sheer drops, notably from the radomes. In the following section we describe the site in detail, beginning with a brief description of the site's origins, construction phases and its occupants, before progressing to a detailed description and analysis of the buildings themselves.

3 The Teufelsberg, history and context

Introduction

The Teufelsberg lies at the northern end of a large area of historic woodland, the Grunewald, bounded to the west by the River Havel and to its north by the gentle valley of the River Spree. To its northwest is the medieval city of Spandau and to the east the historic suburb of Charlottenburg and beyond the city of Berlin (Figure 3.1).

At the beginning of the 19th century the Grunewald was called Spandauer Forst, and most of it was already divided into a series of regular blocks, Jagen, 400m × 800m (Starck 1810). A century later the Grunewald was a royal forest and marked the western extent of the rapidly expanding city, its suburbs served by new fast commuter lines, the Schnellbahn (S-Bahn), one of whose lines bisects the forest (Bibliographisches Institut 1913) (Figure 3.2).

At the beginning of the 20th century an ambitious public road, doubling as a racetrack, was planned, the Automobil Verkehrs und Übungs Strasse (AVUS). Its course was to the west of, and parallel with, the S-Bahn. Work started on this in 1913 and was completed by 1921. But far more significant changes were planned in the 1930s, when the National Socialist Party dreamed of remodelling Berlin as Germania, a classically inspired capital of a Greater Germany. This of course never materialised, although elements were completed. For example, immediately to the north of the Teufelsberg is the stadium built for the 1936 Olympics, and to the northeast were the great exhibition halls of the Deutschland Halle and the Funkturm, the tower of the earlier 1920s radio station (Figure 3.3).

At the northern end of the Grunewald, and beneath what is now the Teufelsberg, the architect Albert Speer planned to build a new university, including an army technical institute, Wehrtechnische Fakultät der Technisen Hochschule. Adolf Hitler laid the foundation stone in November 1937 and by the outbreak of war in 1939, it had risen to two storeys, but was unfinished and was used for the storage of ammunition and explosives until being finally

Figure 3.1 The Teufelsberg seen from the Grunewald Turm
Source: Angus Boulton

Im Grunewald.

Figure 3.2 The Grunewald, 1906
Source: private collection

Figure 3.3 Allied air reconnaissance photograph of the Grunewald in March 1944.
To the top is the 1936 Olympic Stadium and in the bottom left is the
partially completed army technical institute

Source: private collection

destroyed by allied bombing in 1945 (v Bronewski nd; Stache 2000). Wartime and immediately post-war aerial photographs show the building comprising parallel ranges to form a square fortress-like building, 120m square,
with projecting corner towers to the east (RCAHMS TW2972 J/357 frame
3240, 20 February 1944, Berlin December 1953; AIR 34/576; www.google.
co.uk/intl/en_uk/earth/).

In wartime Berlin, the Grunewald was a place of escape from an increasingly bomb-damaged city, but it also took on a more sinister function as
its railway station became one of the main places of forced deportations to
the east (Read and Fisher 1993, 91). It was also the scene of one of the last

actions of the war as the left flank of Rybalko's Soviet 3rd Guards Tank Army swept through the woods in its drive towards the city centre to engage the remnants of the 18th Panzer Grenadier Division. By Saturday 28 April 1945, Colonel Gragunsky, commander of the Soviet 55th Guards Tank Brigade, had established an operational base at the northern end of the Grunewald in the Eichkamp area (Read and Fisher 1993, 411; Beevor 2002, 324; Altner 2005, 166). Following the post-war division of the city, administratively, the Teufelsberg lay in the district of Wilmersdorf within the British zone.

The city and the mound

In the immediate post-war years, woodland provided an important source of fuel for Berliners. It was also chosen as one of the most convenient places to dump unusable rubble from the clearance of an estimated 88,000 bomb-damaged ruins across the city. With huge losses amongst Germany's male population, the *trümmerfrauen*, or rubble women, carried out much of the clearance work, with large amounts of the debris moved by temporary light railways. The Teufelsberg is one of these rubble mounds, sited here presumably to hide the half-completed and now bomb-damaged institute, and to use its foundations to give the mound stability (Anderson 2017). As the mound grew, it therefore covered the part-finished institute and the regular grid of woodland tracks, covering Jagen 110, 111 and 112. The previously straight Teufelseechaussee was diverted in an eastwards arc and an irregular series of paths developed around the mound (Figure 3.4). The dumping of rubble continued for about

Figure 3.4 Teufelseechaussee. The modern road curves around the dumped rubble of the Teufelsberg and has replaced the original straight track

Source: authors

25 years with the mound finally closed in December 1971 (Beckmann et al. 2011, 21–22).

The name of the Teufelsberg, or Devil's Mountain, created from unusable wartime rubble, might seem particularly appropriate, but was in fact derived from a small natural lake, the Teufelsee, that lies to its south in the Grunewald. In the 1950s the mound's official name was 'Restschuttekippe am Teufelsberg' (Beckmann et al. 2011, 13) and on contemporary maps it was simply marked as a rubble dumping ground. By the early 1960s it was named the Trümmerberg, a name it kept until at least the middle of the decade, before it became generally known as the Teufelsberg (Schaffman und Kluge c1961; Schaffman und Kluge c1965). Unofficially, to Berliners, it was Mont Klamotte, from the local dialect word for brick or stone. Following construction of the listening post, the Teufelsberg acquired a new set of names and aliases in keeping with its clandestine activities, and the tendency amongst military personnel to reduce any long word to an acronym. It therefore now also became the 'T-Berg', 'TB', 'The Hill', 'Spooky Hill', 'Asylum on the Hill' or 'Phallus in Wonderland'. Officially, to the Americans the facility was known as Field Station Berlin, and after the Intelligence and Security Command (INSCOM) took charge it simply became Site 3. To the East Germans it was known as 'America's Big Ear' (Wolf 1998, 294). In the 1980s, perhaps in an attempt to disguise its true function, a contemporary tourist map marked it as 'Mil radaranl', military radar anlage (complex) (RV Reise-und Verkehrsverlag nd c.1980s).

In the divided city of the Cold War, the Grunewald's green space became especially important to West Berliners, being surrounded by the communist East and unable to easily leave the city. The huge rubble mound had two summits: the southern one was to be occupied by the listening post, while that and the one to the north became popular recreational spots offering winter skiing and sledging – there was a ski-lift, two ski-jumps and a judges' tower built on the northern and north-eastern faces of the Teufelsberg, playing host to the 1986 Slalom World Championships. Two toboggan runs were also carved into the western face of the Teufelsberg, one at 548m long (Behling and Jüttemann 2011, 14). The adjacent S-Bahn and the AVUS also acquired a new significance as the permitted access routes into West Berlin leading to the rail border crossing at Griebnitzsee and autobahn border at Checkpoint Bravo, Dreilinden. The Grunewald also provided an important training area for the American occupation troops, and other military facilities included a now dismantled ammunition dump.

Construction phases

The construction of the listening post on the Teufelsberg divides into three main phases:

1   1961–1966 – Beginnings
2   Late 1960s to early 1970s – Permanence
3   1980s – Consolidation

1961–1966

From about 1961, the first military surveillance detachments on the Teufelsberg relied on mobile equipment and cabins, which by late 1962 had evolved into a large camp of conjoined trailers and vans (Figures 3.5 & 3.6).

By the middle of the following year a large inflatable dome had been added to cover a rotating radar head with six semi-permanent huts radiating from its base. By 1964 most of the mobile trailers had disappeared and the

Figure 3.5 The Teufelsberg, 1962. This shows the first phase of occupation when the station comprised interlinked trucks and trailers

Source: Allied Museum Berlin

Figure 3.6 The Teufelsberg, 1963–1964. As the site developed, an inflatable dome
was built over the main antenna and further temporary cabins added

Source: Allied Museum Berlin

first permanent buildings had been constructed (TNA: FO 1060/4690, 20
December 1963). To the west a permanent, metal, 12-sided tower [1425]
with a radome was added along with a three-storey brick building [1437A]
between it and the pneumatic dome. This later functioned as a central communications building. More single-storey huts were also added.

Late 1960s to early 1970s

In the wider Cold War standoff between East and West, the late 1960s and
early 1970s marked a period of improved relations – détente. Specifically
the election of Willy Brandt as West German chancellor in October 1969
was the beginning of new relationships with the states of eastern Europe –
Ostpolitik. Despite this thaw in international relations at this time, Field
Station Berlin embarked on a major redevelopment programme, codenamed
Project Filman (Figure 3.7) (Beckmann et al. 2011, 49).

   Planning for this began in late 1968 when the United States announced it
wished to requisition another three areas on the Teufelsberg covering 2816

Figure 3.7 The Teufelsberg, 1971. This view shows the site after the completion of the ambitious Project Filman

Source: Allied Museum Berlin

square metres (TNA: FO 1060/5191, 10 December 1968). Two massive operations buildings were constructed: a two-storey building [1455] for the British, and a large three-storey building [1458] capped by a tower and three radomes for the Americans. Parts of the British building were operational by June 1972 and the United States' building by November of that year (Bowman 1997). To cater for the increase in personnel, a new Dining Facility and store [1455] was built to the southwest, and to the east a heating plant [1456] and a powerhouse [1457]. Shortly after the completion of Project Filman in 1972, a new guardroom [1454] was added and to its rear a covered and raised corridor linking the main operational buildings [1425], [1437A], [1455] and [1458]. Around this time a 120m mast was constructed. Also during the mid-1970s an experimental surveillance device, 'Jambalaya', was installed at the western end of the site. It occupied the site of a later tower of the same name [1465]. Between 1978 and 1982, minor additions to the facility included the construction of a document-shredding building [1469] and two electrical switch rooms [1467] and [1468]. To the east a large electrical transformer house was built [1466] and extensions were made to the Dining Facility [1455].

1980s

These were a prelude to another massive building campaign with the commissioning of the large double-storey Teufelsberg II, or Building U [1475], in late 1982. This was opened on 14 August 1982 by Wing Command C I Johnson, Commanding Officer 26 Signals Unit, and Colonel Cloyd H Pfister, Officer Commanding Field Station Berlin (TNA: AIR 29/4927, August 1982). The building was officially accepted in October; around this time there was a noticeable spike in visitors to the unit from HQ RAF Germany, GCHQ and the electronic manufacturers Racal Decca, all no doubt concerned with fitting out the new building (TNA: AIR 29/4927, October 1982, November 1982). The earlier operations buildings were probably refurbished, including a new plant room [1458A] (Figure 3.8).

The political context for this work was a worsening of East-West relations prompted by factors such as the Soviet invasion of Afghanistan in 1979 and its deployment of the new SS20 missile system in eastern Europe. In America, the Reagan administration entered office in January 1981 with a mission to 're-arm America', with defence spending rising by 50 percent during the president's first term (Isaacs and Downing 1998, 334). Around the same time, other minor modifications included a

Figure 3.8 The Teufelsberg in its final form during the late 1980s

Source: Allied Museum Berlin

new plant room on the southern side of the British building [1455] and to its north a document incinerator [1455B]. The Guardroom [1454] was also extended and rest area and store area [1498] added. In 1987, the last building to be added was the Jambalaya tower [1465], which, as we have seen, replaced an earlier device of the same name (Beckmann et al. 2011, 47–56; Bowman 1997).

By the late 1980s there were three main antenna types on the Teufelsberg, for radio signal sending and receiving, sending and receiving data trans-missions and radar-receiving. Targets for this equipment included military communications and cables, telex machines, telephone calls and satellite communications (Bowman 1997).

American presence

Standing about 120m high, the Teufelsberg is the tallest of Berlin's artifi-cial rubble hills. Around 1960, the United States Army was seeking new interception sites and quickly exploited the potential of this vantage point as an electronic surveillance post. By July 1961, the top of Teufelsberg had been requisitioned and was the centre for United States electronic eaves-dropping, and two years later personnel numbers had risen to a couple of hundred (Holbrook 2008, 61). James Holbrook, a specialist Russian lin-guist with the 78th Special Operations Unit who arrived at the Teufelsberg in 1963, has described the unit's working pattern. Personnel worked four, eight-hour shifts, known as 'tricks'. One team worked a day shift for six days, another team worked 'swings' or 'eves' and another worked 'mids' from midnight to 8am. After a 48 or 72 hour break, a team changed its shift hours, so one team would always be on a rest break (Holbrook 2008, 61). Rob Pellington, who served there at the same time, described how loud music was constantly played over the loudspeaker system to thwart any attempts to listen to conversations on the hill (Pellington nd). This has also been described as happening at ISCOM Site 4, to the southeast of the Teufelsberg. Language specialists included speakers of Russian, German, Polish and Czechoslovakian (Eichner and Dobbert 1997, 227). Most had passed through the Defence Language Institute at Monterey, California, hence their being referred to commonly as the 'Monterey Marys'. Their technical colleagues were trained in Morse code and electronics at Fort Devens, Massachusetts, and were known as the 'Devens Dollies' (Cooper 2002, 8).

In the early 1960s, the Teufelsberg was still a rubble-strewn hill with just two permanent buildings. One building housed technical equipment, while the other was a mess hall. The specialists initially worked in mobile com-munications vans equipped with radio receivers, tape recorders and desks.

These were later replaced by semi-permanent structures (Holbrook 2008, 62). Routine work at this time included the interception and transcription of Soviet communications. In the event of war, the unit was also trained in 'imitative communications deception' (ICD) and with the potential to break into enemy communications networks to spread disinformation and false commands (Holbrook 2008, 67). Occasionally, the routine daily tricks could be broken by periods of intense activity. In March 1964, a United States Air Force RB-66 reconnaissance aircraft strayed into East German airspace and was shot down. In the hours and days following this incident, real-time information on the Soviet's actions was crucial to the West's response (Holbrook 2008, 68–70). In the late 1960s, an example of the application of intercepted data was the analysis of standard East German telegrams to soldiers of the Nationale Volksarmee. At the USASA's Target Exploitation (TAREX) in Frankfurt, a computer programme was devised to analyse these data to reveal the order of battle of the East German army (www.cdstrand.com/areas/usasaeur.htm)

By 1966, all the US Army Security Agency's mobile units were moved to the Teufelsberg and the unit was redesignated the 54th Special Operations Command. A year later it became Field Station Berlin. In 1977, the United States Army Security Agency became the Intelligence and Security Command (INSCOM), and this unit became the United States Army Field Station Berlin. By the late 1970s, its Communications Centre was known as USM-620K, indicating it was a detachment of the main Communications Centre USM-620 at Andrews Barracks. Towards the end of its history, when the communications centre at Andrews Barracks was closed, the Teufelsberg Field Station became USM-5 (Pilzak 2000). By the time of its closure in 1992, the Teufelsberg housed hundreds of millions of dollars' worth of surveillance equipment and was able to intercept electronic emissions within a radius of at least 300km (Eichner and Dobbert 1997, 225; Herrington 1999, 68). During the 1980s the number of personnel here varied between 1300 and 1500, of which around 1000 were Americans and the remainder British (Bowman 1997). Amongst this number were linguists, analysts and researchers from the National Security Agency, as well as air force personnel (Wyden 1989, 114). A more detailed list of United States' units appears in the inset box.

In addition to the Teufelsberg, the United States operated a number of listening stations along the inner German border. The one at Wobeck, Niedersachsen, to the southwest of the Helmstadt border crossing, was of particular significance to the operations in Berlin and was operated by Bravo Company, Support Battalion, a Berlin Army Security Agency detachment (Bowman 1997).

United States Army units based at the Teufelsberg (after Prock 1992)

January 1951 – F Detachment, Field Station 8606 relocated from Herzogenaurach (Herzo Base), Bavaria, to Berlin

April 1952 – E Detachment Field Station 8606 relocated to Berlin

June 1952 – E Detachment status changed from temporary duty to Duty Station

1953 – Detachment E renamed Detachment F

1 July 1953 – Detachment C Field Station 8606 joins F Detachment

26 March 1954 – Detachment B headquarters ASA Europe established in Berlin

September 1954 – Detachments F and C attached for administrative and logistic purposes

1954 – Detachment A 302nd Communications Reconnaissance Battalion established to control all these elements plus two small ASA teams Team 6 and Team 620J1

1955 – Detachment B US Army Europe reorganised as a provisional company

1 November 1955 – 9539th Technical Service Unit relocated from Fort Myer, Virginia, to Berlin and assigned to ASA and designated 22nd ASA Detachment

1 January 1957 – redesignated 260th ASA Detachment

15 October 1957 – 280th Army Security Agency takes charge of USASA assets in Berlin. The company comprised seven officers, two warrant officers and 136 enlisted men, with its headquarters at Andrews Barracks.

15 June 1961 – redesignated 78th Special Operations Unit

July 1961 – 78th SOU first locates mobile equipment on the Teufelsberg

November 1963 – a semi-permanent site is in place at the Teufelsberg

22 June 1966 – 78th SOU redesignated 54th Special Operations Command

March 1967 – Internally organised into Headquarters and Service Company, Company A and Company B

15 December 1967 – redesignated ASA Field Station Berlin

April 1969 to September 1972 Project Filman – permanent facilities created

1 April 1977 – redesignated US Army Field Station Berlin US Army Intelligence and Security Command (INSCOM) – motto 'On Watch'

Other units based at the Teufelsberg
National Security Agency
6912 Electronic Security Group USAF

**Principal United States Air Force electronic surveillance
units in Berlin**

July 1951 Det D 2nd Radio Squadron Mobile (Det D 7350th Air
  Base Complement Sq)
1951 Det 24, 2nd Radio Squadron Mobile (Det D 7350th Air
  Base Complement Sq)
1 January 1954 Flight A, 2nd Radio Squadron Mobile
1 October 1954 Det 1 85th Radio Squadron Mobile
8 May 1955 Det 1 6914th Radio Squadron Mobile
1 September 1956 Det 1 6910th Radio Squadron Mobile
1 July 1959 6912th Radio Squadron Mobile
1 July 1963 6912th Security Squadron
1 August 1979 6912th Electronic Security Group
15 July 1988 690th Electronic Security Wing
12 June 1991 690th Electronic Security Group
7350th Air Base Squadron was the unit responsible for the operation of Tempelhof Central Airport
16 January 1992 The US units were inactivated

British presence

In August 1961, access to East Berlin was closed by the construction of the
Wall and with it the ability of western intelligence agencies to readily contact
agents in East Germany. British intelligence efforts in Berlin had also been
seriously compromised by the treachery of George Blake, a Soviet agent
within the British Secret Intelligence Service. After suffering these twin
blows, signals intelligence assumed a far greater prominence. Soon after the
Americans established a presence on the Teufelsberg, a small detachment
of British linguists was sent on testing duties. This occupation became permanent in 1963, and coinciding with the move to Hangar 4 at Gatow, the
Polish linguists were established in a wooden hut on the Teufelsberg. Construction of purpose-built British facilities began within the American compound in summer 1964, and in addition to the hut included at least one lattice
tower (TNA: FO 1060/4690, 7 August 1964). Equipment in this building
included British-made EMI RE 301 military-grade recorders, although these
were replaced in 1969 by Telefunken TL85 recorders (TNA: AIR 29/3881,

November 1969). During the late 1960s, more RAF personnel were moved to the Teufelsberg, where they worked alongside members of the Royal Corps of Signals and personnel from the Government Communications Headquarters (GCHQ), Cheltenham (www.jao.delboys.com/26SU.htm).

RAF signals units at RAF Gatow

No 3 Detachment 365 Signals Unit (1951–1953)
No 3 Signals Detachment from No.5 Signals Wing (February 1953 365 Signals Unit renamed 5 Signals Wing)
No 5 Signals Detachment from No.5 Signals Wing
No 1 (Signals) Wing Detachment
No 5 (Signals) Wing Detachment
No 2 Sqdn 5 Signals Wing
26 Signals Unit (1966 No 5 Signals Wing was renamed 26 Signals Unit)
29 February 1992 British operations ceased

By May 1968, planning was underway to move the majority of the British personnel to the Teufelsberg, project code EEI 8153 (TNA: AIR 29/3881, May 1968, October 1970). Work on Building M [1455] began in 1969 and by spring 1971 an RAF radio engineering unit was at work fitting out the new building. The initial work was soon completed and the first units became operational in the building on 28 June 1971, when the wooden hut was abandoned (TNA: AIR 29/4332, May 1971, June 1971). Installation of new equipment under EEI 8153 continued for the remainder of 1971 including the setting up of equipment for 13 Signals Regiment (TNA: AIR 29/4332, November 1971). By January 1972, phase 1 of EEI 8153 was complete and the facility was commissioned and handed over to the operating units, although work continued on phase 2 until September. The remainder of the personnel who were posted to the Teufelsberg arrived in late September and the RAF assumed full control of the building in mid-November (TNA: AIR 29/4332, January 1972, September 1972). Coinciding with the commissioning of Building M, Wing Commander A E Schofield was appointed as the commanding officer of 26 Signals Unit in July 1971 and remained to oversee its transition to a fully operational unit by July 1973 (TNA: AIR 29/4332, July 1971, July 1973) (Figure 3.9).

Photographs were taken during the fitting out work and give a good impression of the character of the building's interior and equipment in use

Figure 3.9 Wing Commander A E Schofield, Officer Commanding 26 Signals Unit
1971–1973, reputedly in his office at the Teufelsberg

Source: J Schofield

during the early 1970s. Unfortunately, the original prints were contaminated by asbestos and now only photocopies survive (TNA: AIR 29/4332). The rooms were utilitarian, with square linoleum tiles. Room divisions were mainly formed from prefabricated panels, which allowed for some flexibility and reconfiguration of the building to meet changing operational requirements. Most of the panels were plain, and to prevent observation from the corridors, many had ceiling-height window units. The rooms were fitted with suspended ceilings and circular lights mounted in the ceiling panels. Another feature of this phase was at least one screened room, essentially a Faraday cage, to prevent the escape of electronic emissions. Equipment installed at this date included British-manufactured Ferrograph Series 7 reel-to-reel tape recorders (Figure 3.10).

Visible numbers indicate that at least 94 of these machines were installed. Each of these was a single workstation with separate swivel chairs and, a feature of contemporary working life, shared ashtrays set into the desks (Figure 3.11). Elsewhere in the building were Siemens T100 teleprinters (Figure 3.12). These machines were used to send typed messages and could also be used to decipher incoming signals onto perforated tape and then onto

Figure 3.10 Ferrograph Series 7 tape recorders installed in 1971, copied from the only known surviving photocopy

Source: TNA: AIR 29/4332

Figure 3.11 Detailed view of voice operator positions and Ferrograph Series 7 tape recorders installed in 1971, copied from the only known surviving photocopy

Source: TNA: AIR 29/4332

Figure 3.12 Siemens T100 teleprinters installed in 1971, copied from the only
            known surviving photocopy
Source: TNA: AIR 29/4332

plain language on ordinary paper. Listening to the sound of a single machine
(www.youtube.com/watch?v=pUxVJEocME8, accessed 7 June 2014) gives
an impression of how noisy any rooms housing them would have been.
Furnishings were spartan and generally restricted to steel-framed desks and
swivel armchairs. In addition to the British-manufactured equipment, the
German firm of Rohde and Schwarz was commissioned to install the aerials on the roof of Building M. This included a tall mast at the western end
of the building known as the 'Bean Pole' that is visible on a contemporary
air photograph (Figure 3.7) (TNA: AIR 29/4332, September 1972, October
1972). Generally, and as discussed in the following chapter, there was little
operational contact between the British and American teams, and personnel rarely entered one another's buildings, although occasionally British
linguists were loaned to the Americans.

RAF Gatow retained administrative responsibility for further construction work at the Teufelsberg and its operational records provide some information on later modifications to the building. In July 1975, major projects
were approved to improve the disposal of classified waste and modifications to Room 117 (TNA: AIR 28/2016, July 1975). Further improvements

were documented in 1979 when work was completed on workshop lighting, and over the next year or so the computer floor and screened cage were extended. A 'DSS Installation' was also completed, which may refer to a digital satellite system and the dishes installed at the southeast corner of Building M (TNA: AIR 28/2215, August 1979; March 1980; June 1980; November 1980) (Figures 5.37 and 5.39).

Technical equipment used at RAF Gatow and the Teufelsberg

This list details some of the equipment used at RAF Gatow and the Teufelsberg. It is incomplete, and information on some of the surveillance and recording equipment remains classified. The RAF Signals Museum, RAF Halton and the Duxford Radio Society have examples of some of this equipment, and the Bundeswehr Museum, Dresden, displays a 1980s VAX computer.

RAF Gatow, Hanbury Block

Late 1950s

> RAF Telefunken control consoles
> Grundig tape recorders
> Royal Signals
> Eddystone 770 Receiver 19 valve 19–165 MHz AM & FM receiver
> D90 – reader for scrambled Soviet voice and cipher traffic
> British army VHF receiver

Source – www.langeleben.co.uk/Brian%20Patchett/brian_patchett_page1.htm, accessed 7 January 2016

RAF Gatow, Hangar 4

Late 1960s

> Rohde & Schwarz Automatic Direction Finder Type NP4 (October 1967)
> RVT 195 (CR Direction Finding) withdrawn from service (November 1967)
> Hewlett-Packard video recorder HP3950 (January 1969)
> Ferrograph Series 7 – reel-to-reel tape recorders (February 1969)

CEI Receiver 521A (fitted June 1969)
Digital Counter DRO 290A (fitted June 1969)
Replaced obsolete receiver R216 (June 1969) Transistor radio
    19–157 MHz in 5 Bands AM/FM/CW receiver
RE301 Recorder (ex-Teufelsberg) (November 1969)
Replaced by T85 KL recorder
Marconi Display Unit S3001 (April 1970)

Source – AIR 29/3881 No.26 Signals Unit, RAF Gatow September 1966–
December 1970

Ampex VR 650 video recorder – obsolete (January 1971)
Hewlett-Packard counter – 5233L (March 1971)

Source – TNA: AIR 29/4332 No.26 Signals Unit, RAF Gatow January 1971–
December 1975

Late 1980s

VAX computer

Source – pers. comm.

Teufelsberg

1960s

RE301 Recorder (Moved to Gatow) (November 1969)

Source – TNA: AIR 29/3881 No.26 Signals Unit, RAF Gatow September
1966–December 1970

1970s

Ferrograph Series 7 – reel-to-reel tape recorders
Ampex Reproducer 445/B2 (March 1972)
Replaced Ampex 352 S
Teletype T28 (March 1972)
Siemens T100 teleprinters

Source – TNA: AIR 29/4332 No.26 Signals Unit, RAF Gatow January 1971–
December 1975

Summary

Building on the earlier history of intelligence-gathering activities in Cold War Berlin, this chapter has outlined the history of first American and then British presence on the Teufelsberg, and some detail of the equipment used to conduct their activities. In the next chapter, we will present the archaeological methodology used to examine the site and some of the rationale for using an archaeological approach for such a recently used and abandoned building. The following chapter will see that method applied to the buildings comprising the Teufelsberg, as we experienced it in 2011.

4   Archaeological investigation: methods and approaches

Archaeologies of the Cold War

Applying archaeological methods to sites and buildings of recent date is nothing new (eg Harrison and Schofield 2010, for examples). Archaeological methods have also previously been applied to Cold War sites and landscape (eg Schofield and Cocroft 2007, for examples). But there is novelty in the approach adopted here, and in the subject to which the methods are applied in this case. This chapter will therefore examine the degree to which these methods are novel, and the extent to which, through their innovation, they shed new light on a previously underexplored aspect of Cold War heritage: signals intelligence. In short, what is new about this study of the Teufelsberg; how innovative is it; and does it provide a blueprint for the archaeological study of other comparable 'secret' installations? This is a topic shrouded in secrecy, for obvious reasons relating to past and ongoing national security. As we have seen, documents that describe these sites and the activities conducted within them are not available for critical historical analysis. Similarly, and as was discovered in this project, former employees and intelligence officers are bound by a lifelong commitment to confidentiality through the Official Secrets Act. Yet an archaeological approach – investigating and closely analysing the buildings, where these survive and are accessible – is one that can reveal new insight through its close and critical attention to detail. Furthermore, with the current emphasis on intelligence gathering within an increasingly uncertain political arena, one might argue that such an approach to understanding secret installations has particular relevance at this time.

In many ways the methods adopted for use at the Teufelsberg have been developed and used elsewhere. Characterisation and its integration with buildings recording was a methodology adopted for use at an older but equally iconic intelligence-gathering site, the Government Code and Cipher School at Bletchley Park. This was the place where information handling and analysis was first carried out on an industrial scale, using electro-mechanical technology and the earliest programmable computers (Lake et al. 2006, 49–57). By the time of the survey, significant time had passed post-abandonment and the historical importance of the site was firmly established in the popular consciousness. Much had been written, and many documents were available for scrutiny. Of the Cold War era, much has been documented of the surviving fabric, in large part the result of national surveys such as that undertaken by English Heritage (Cocroft and Thomas 2003) and the Danish Heritage Agency (Stenak et al. 2013). But these surveys have also revealed gaps, either related to categories of site which were mobile and thus highly ephemeral and poorly documented, or where they were secretive and for which any archival sources remain classified. These latter sites either remain inaccessible or in use, or their location remains unknown due to lack of published information. The Teufelsberg is a rare and perhaps unique example of a significant Cold War intelligence-gathering installation which is both known and accessible. It exists in plain sight, as it has done since the mid-1960s, within a modern capital city at the heart of the Cold War's geopolitical landscape. The site was stripped after the end of the Cold War, to prevent others from obtaining information about the allies' capacity for information gathering. Only subtle traces remain, traces that developed archaeological methods are well suited to recording.

Field methods

Our archaeological approach to documenting and interpreting what remains at the Teufelsberg is based on standard archaeological approaches to any extant site, with an initial phase of documentary-based research, a reconnaissance and then more detailed characterisation and survey to determine the logic and configuration of space and how the site was used over time by its occupants. This does require the survival of buildings to determine construction phases, plan form and use. Although highly altered since its Cold War occupation ended (see Chapter 6), the buildings do survive, comprising far more detail than might be assumed, and more than at the majority of earlier archaeological sites.

In studying the Teufelsberg, survey time was limited, although for most buildings basic floor plans were available and made the process significantly quicker than beginning from scratch (after Beckmann et al. 2011). Using these floor plans as a starting point (and like a conventional map, in the field) our approach was to survey each entire building, room by room, corridor by corridor, and all of the spaces around each building, using conventional field archaeological survey methods. The survey essentially followed the guidelines for a Historic England Level 2 record; the building was viewed, described and photographed, with limited drawing undertaken for some specific features. However, the degree of research and analysis required to build understanding and interpretation was more compatible with higher levels of survey (Historic England 2016, 25–27). From this survey work, building and room functions were established and mapped based on evidence of remaining fittings and fixtures, creating a broad characterisation for each of the buildings and the rooms and spaces within them (Figures 4.1, 4.2, 5.29 and 5.30).

Our documentation included the creation of 'characterisation' maps accompanied by field notes and photographs. As well as our own 'record' photographs, the artist Angus Boulton accompanied us during the week of fieldwork and took additional images which capture the overarching character of the site and our engagement with it. As stated earlier, the interiors of many buildings were completely dark. Most had been stripped when the station was abandoned, and in the intervening years were subject to further stripping and vandalism. These were dangerous spaces therefore, strewn with rubble and with randomly placed holes in the floor. Nevertheless, the information

Figure 4.1 To understand the operation of the buildings, rooms were characterised by function, appearance and access routes

Source: authors

Figure 4.2 Measuring features on the roof of the RAF building 1455
Source: authors

recorded was sufficient to create a broad picture of functional areas and blocks of associated rooms in spite of these difficulties.

The Teufelsberg is a source of fascination for urban explorers. Many, often illicit, visits are documented on the web and now offer a historic record of the site at various points in time. These photographic documentations and recorded memories have also been used to complement field observations. Dust samples were taken from several locations around the site and subject to scientific examination.

Often with sites of the Cold War period, field investigations play a promi-nent role as documentation and oral testimony is either restricted to mun-dane aspects of the site's functionality and use, or is absent entirely, either having been destroyed or classified. In this case of the Teufelsberg some oral testimony is available online, and where relevant this is referred to in the text. In terms of documentation, some of the Operational Records Books of signals units based at the Teufelsberg are accessible although with key details redacted. Perfectly capturing the spirit of the project, a Freedom of Information request submitted in 2011 produced the following response, highlighting the sensitivities still associated with the site, and activities con-ducted here:

> the MOD neither confirms nor denies whether it holds any additional information within the scope of your request by virtue of Section 23(5) (Information supplied by, or relating to bodies dealing with security matters) and Section 24(2) (National Security), which is a qualified exemption. Section 23 is an absolute exemption and does not require a public interest test to be conducted. To the extent Section 24(2) applies, we have concluded that in all the circumstances of the case, the public interest in maintaining the exclusion of the duty to confirm or deny outweighs the public interest in confirming whether any information is held. Confirmation or denial of whether there is or is not security or intelligence interest and/or capability could be exploited by individuals or organisations with consequent damage to national security.

A twist, however, is that documentation is available from the very source that operatives at the Teufelsberg sought to eavesdrop. A summary of infor-mation contained in a Stasi file dated 1978 included clear indications that some understanding of the site and its capabilities had been achieved. For example, the existence of the location of the Teufelsberg had been known since 1966, while from 1971 it had become clear that the '26th signal unit' was using the site. From 1978 it was known that 26 Signals Unit was a highly confidential special unit of the RAF, whose task was 'electronic spy-ing' against the GDR and other socialist countries. This fact was described as proven by:

• Conversations by British officers
• High security standard of the buildings
• Big computer systems at Hangar 4

- The composition of the staff, with many being proficient in the Slavic languages, including Russian and Czech
- The fact that all visitors to the buildings are 'classified'
- The direct subordination of 26 Signals Unit under GCHQ Cheltenham

The report describes how the work at Teufelsberg functioned, notably that working spaces of British and Americans were separated, the Americans were solely responsible for guarding the building, and that several times a day there were VW buses transporting 'sound record mediums' (resembling rolls of film) from the Teufelsberg to Hangar 4 – where it is assumed the records were interpreted/evaluated.

Summary

The focus of this project is archaeological, with an emphasis on reading and interpreting the field remains that have survived the various phases of stripping out. The work demonstrates the validity of such an archaeological approach even in situations where sites have been 'cleared'. Some limited documentation (written and oral) is available and has been used to support field interpretation. Various additional sources provide a soundtrack to the project and can be located online; these sources include contemporary music played at or inspired by the site (see Chapter 7), real-time sound recordings of the site, which effectively document its degradation, and films of the machinery used at the Teufelsberg.

5 Site description

Site layout

By 1960, the Teufelsberg had risen to 115m, with a level, irregular-shaped summit accessed by an unsurfaced, winding track from the Teufel-seechaussee. Around its edges, to minimise erosion and aid the establishment of vegetation, small terraces were cut in to its slopes. From 1970 until 1984, some of these terraces supported a vineyard for the production of Wilmers-dorfer Teufelsströpfchen or Wilmersdorf's Devil's Drops (Behling and Jüt-temann 2011, 17). Over the following decades the hill was sculpted to create roadways, car parks and level building platforms. By the late 1980s the site covered an irregular-shaped area on the summit with a maximum extent of about 300m × 200m (Figure 5.1).

Visiting the site today, a post and wire mesh fence topped by barbed wire surrounds the outer perimeter of the entire site, which was originally illuminated by lamp standards. Internally, double fence lines further protected the more sensitive areas, also creating an internal patrol path. These fences defined three broad zones. In the southwest corner a single fence protected the main car park and main access track. To the east was a technical compound surrounded by an outer double fence, which was further separated from the main western operations area by a double fence that enclosed this area. Within this area movement was further restricted by a fence from the north side of the British building [1455], creating a compound to its south. At the northern end of the site was another gate-restricted access to the rear of the main operations building [1458]. What follows is a detailed description of the site, as it existed in summer 2011.

The main gate

From Teufelseechaussee a winding double-laned road led to a single, large, electrically operated sliding gate that controlled access into the Teufelsberg (Figure 5.2).

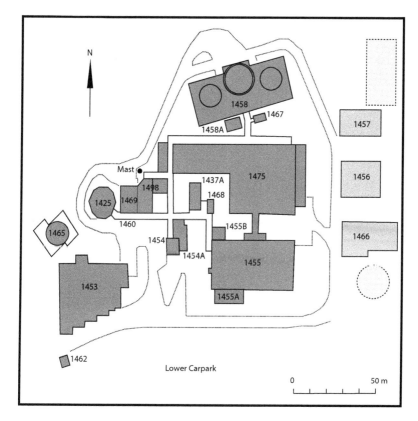

Figure 5.1 Plan of the Teufelsberg

1425 – Building D, the Arctic Tower, Search Tower
1437A – Building H, communications
1453 – Building L – mess
1454 – Building B – Guardroom
1454A – Security Police rooms
1455 – Building M – British building
1455A – Air-conditioning plant
1455B – Incinerator
1456 – Building F, heating pant, demolished
1457 – Building K1, K2, transformer, demolished
1458 – Building G, Main US Operations Building
1458A – Building H, plant room
1460 – Corridor
1462 – Main gate guard post
1465 – Building N, Jambalaya tower
1466 – Building P, electrical switchgear, demolished
1467 – Building R, electrical switchgear
1468 – Building S, electrical switch room
1469 – Building T, paper shredding and pulping
1475 – Teufelsberg II, US and British computing and analysts building
1498 – Bar and storerooms

Figure 5.2 Main gate to the Teufelsberg. Beyond the gate the track split into two
Source: authors

Immediately to the north on the slope is a wooden watchtower (Figure 5.3). Beyond the gate the track split into two, the lower arm giving access to a large lower car park and the upper arm to the main part of the site, including the listening post. At the point where the track separated is a small, square guard post [1462] (Figure 5.4).

This is faced in red brick laid to stretcher bond with vertically set brick window lintels. It has a flat roof and on one corner is an air-conditioning unit. The post has large, triple-glazed-armour windows set in metal frames on all sides, and to the rear is a single full-length glazed door. To the front are two spotlights that shone towards the main gate. Most of the hut's interior fittings have been removed, but telephone points, cabling and electrical sockets remain attached to its walls, and adjacent to the door is a double rifle rack (Figure 5.5). Externally, there is a metal pole with four arms that probably supported observation mirrors. In front of the post was a small garden, now represented by untended plants.

To control access beyond the guard post, to either side, set into the tracks and spanning their full widths, are rising metal barriers which slotted into steel pillars to either end (Figure 5.6). The lower track led to the main car

Figure 5.3 Wooden watchtower overlooking the main gate
Source: Angus Boulton

Figure 5.4 1462, Outer guardroom from the lower car park
Source: Angus Boulton

Figure 5.5 1462, Outer guardroom internal rifle rack
Source: authors

Figure 5.6 Raising barrier on upper road looking back towards the main gate
Source: authors

park, a level terrace cut into the rubble mound and covered by grey paving blocks. Rubble from the excavation of the foundations for an abandoned hotel project in the late 1990s has been dumped on the slope above the car park and covers its east end. At the west end of the car park is a 12-place bicycle rack, manufactured by Gaerner of Duisberg and München. A single outer fence bounds the car park and on its southern side is a double gate. It is unclear if this gate was in regular use, or if it provided the guards with occasional quick access to the perimeter. From the car park a double steel staircase, probably originally covered by canvas, led to the main entrance of the site. Symbolically, two flagpoles, which survive, are positioned at the top of the stairs; one flew the Union Jack and the other the Stars and Stripes.

At the eastern end of the car park is a single white wooden sentry box, its base partly covered by rubble spoil (Figure 5.7). It is topped by a low gable roof and to provide good all-round visibility it has windows on three sides; on the fourth side was a door that is now missing. The sentry box marks the beginning of a double outer fence line, allowing the perimeter to be patrolled by guards and/or dogs (Figure 5.8). Beyond this was a further internal fence.

Figure 5.7 Guard post at the eastern end of the lower car park
Source: Angus Boulton

Figure 5.8 Patrol path around the external double fence line
Source: Angus Boulton

Immediately beyond [1462] on the north side of the upper road was the facility's main stores area beneath the Dining Facility [1453]. After this a minor road headed northwards towards a gate to the west of the main Guardroom [1454] (Figure 5.9). Past the gate were a small car park and a service road skirting around the north of the site. Personnel would normally park

Figure 5.9 To the west of the main guardroom [1462], traces of the sliding gates that passed through the double fence

Source: authors

private cars in the lower car park or its eastern overflow, while duty vehicles might be allowed inside the inner compound.

The eastern compound

Returning to the Dining Facility [1453], the main road continued eastwards immediately to the south of the British building [1455] to a double set of gates leading to the compound surrounding the technical buildings [1456 Heating Plant, 1457 and 1466 Power Houses]. Externally, this compound was protected by three fence lines, and internally a further two fence lines separated it from the main operational buildings to the west. Two double gate entrances permitted trucks to bring equipment and other supplies to the main technical buildings. The northern two of the buildings [1456 and 1457] in this compound were built during the 1969–1972 reconstruction programme. A historic air photograph taken in July 1971 shows both buildings were complete by this date. Building [1456] was originally a heating plant, with a chimney to the south, and [1457] a transformer house. In 1981–1982 the southern building [1466], a new transformer station, was added and [1457] was converted into an air-conditioning plant and [1456] into a pump house for the sprinkler system.

In the late 1990s these buildings were demolished and work began on a soon-to-be-abandoned hotel scheme. To the north a rectangular hole was dug and the foundations for a new building lain, including eight columns. To the south are the large circular foundations of an underground car park. As discussed above, during this work rubble from the excavations was tipped on to the car park and around the lip of the mound. Two large underground fuel storage tanks were also removed and dumped on the eastern side of the hill.

The operational facilities – security and entry control

Personnel of the 6941st Guard Battalion, a unit of uniformed and armed German guards, protected the physical security of the site's perimeter. If required, they might also be supported by the local West Berlin police force. The security of the more sensitive areas was guarded by a 30-strong platoon of United States Army military police personnel based in the main Guardroom [1454] and its annex [1454A]. It was these troops who controlled the main access to the facility. A small number of British RAF police also controlled access into the main British building [1455]. The military police probably also used rooms in the eastern side of [1498]; the metal cages at the entrance were possibly dog kennels. The military police also used the basement beneath the communications building 1437A, which may also have operated as an emergency command post.

The main pedestrian entry into the facility was through the Guardroom [1454]. This is faced in red bricks with steel-framed, double-glazed windows, protected externally by metal roller shutters. On its southern side is a steel frame that originally carried a sign proclaiming 'Teufelsberg'. Entry into the Guardroom was from two sets of stairs on its southern and western sides. Internally is a self-contained metal guard post that controlled entry into the facility. This was entered from a single door to its rear on which was a painted sign stating 'Anmeldung' (Reception) (Figure 5.10).

On the other three sides were armoured glass windows. On the south and west sides are slots for presenting documents, and on the eastern side a flap for passing larger packages. For regular personnel, entry into the facility was on the production of two identification cards that were checked against a name list (Manton 2015, 131). Further access into different parts of the buildings was by number codes, and by the 1980s, with magnetic swipe cards (Beckmann et al. 2011, 178; Behling and Jüttemann 2011, 30). Once

Figure 5.10 1454, Anmeldung (Reception). This guardroom controlled all access to the Teufelsberg

Source: Angus Boulton

past the Guardroom a turnstile gate gave access to the main corridor [1460], and cut-off bolts on the floor indicate its position. Alternatively, on the eastern side is a door with an external cage door that led to the fenced compound surrounding [1455]. It also gave access to the basement of annex [1454A] that housed a telephone exchange supplied by Quante of Wuppertal, with separate terminals allocated to the British and the United States sections (Figure 5.11, 5.12, 5.13).

To the rear of the Guardroom, a door to the right led to a room that may have been used as a police ready room and office. Another door led to the police quarters [1454B]. On the west side of a short access corridor was an armoury secured by steel cage doors. On the opposite side were male and female toilets. At the end of the corridor a sign on the door reads 'PLATOON _ EAD _UARTERS KNOCK BEFORE ENTERING'. Within the room is a mural with the motto 'ASSIST PROTECT DEFEND' (Figure 5.14), and along the north wall a number of electrical cabinets.

Figure 5.11 1454, Guardroom basement telephone exchange

Source: authors

Figure 5.12 1454, Guardroom basement telephone terminal for United States telephone lines

Source: authors

Figure 5.13 1454, Guardroom basement telephone terminal for British telephone lines

Source: authors

Figure 5.14 1454, Guardroom US Security Police mural in the rear crew room

Source: authors

The Guardroom controlled the single entrance to the facility, and beyond it was the main covered corridor [1460]. This is brick built and window-less with an artificial stone terrazzo floor. It is raised about 1.5m above the original ground surface, the under-floor void allowing cabling to be carried around the facility. About 20m from the Guardroom the corridor splits. Directly ahead the corridor continues to provide access to the main US controlled facilities; on its western side is a single door giving access to a Bar [1498]. Returning to the junction to the west the corridor leads to the tower [1425] and the paper-pulping building [1469], while to the east it leads to the communications building [1437A], technical room [1468], the incinerator room [1455B] and the upper floor of the British building [1455]. Immediately after the junction on its north wall are a series of single doors with small rooms behind that housed electrical transformers. Marks on the walls along the corridors indicate the location of brackets for radiators, and of pictures. The number of often closely clustered holes for rawl plugs sug-gests that the configuration of pictures changed over time.

1437A Communications building

This building was constructed about 1965–1966 and is the second oldest surviving building within the facility. It is a three-storey, windowless brick building, measuring 14m x 7m, and is about 7m tall with cast concrete floors and a flat roof. Externally, it has been reclad in light blue pressed-metal panels (Figure 5.15). These are a lighter shade than those used on the rest of the site and were a relatively late addition to the building. The main entrance to the building is on its east side from the later raised internal cor-ridor down a flight of steps, which drop down to the original ground level (Figure 5.16).

The entrance gives access to the building's stairwell. To the right a flight of stairs leads down to the basement with a brown steel door with peephole and on which is painted 'Military Police Shadow Watch'. Internally are two rooms. On the wall of the first is the slogan 'Lead, follow or get the hell out of the way', and to the rear is a room with a suspended floor and ceiling and air conditioning. Returning to the ground floor, the concrete staircase has yellow and blue treads and is protected by its original metal handrail, now painted brown. As part of a later refurbishment the stairwell has been panel lined; where this has been damaged traces of a former yellow, orange and brown horizontal paint scheme is visible. The ground floor is a single large room with two toilet cubicles in its northeast corner. Within this building all the floors are solid and carpet covered. It has been refurbished on at least one occasion and the rooms dry-lined with plasterboard, or plywood panels (Figures 5.17 and 5.18).

Figure 5.15 1437A, communications building. This was clad in bright blue pressed-metal sheets in the late 1980s. To the left is one of the loading doors for the installation of heavy equipment. To its rear is Teufelsberg II [1475], to the right is the British building [1455] and in the lower right corner the main guardroom [1454]

Source: authors

Figure 5.16 1437A, the entrance to the communications building from the later raised corridor to the door at the original ground surface

Source: authors

Figure 5.17 1437A, door to the first floor with a spy hole and the remains of a unit 'zap'

Source: authors

Figure 5.18 1437A. During its earlier phases the building's interior walls were painted in shades of blue, while in its latest phase the working environment was improved with the addition of plasterboards and wooden panelling

Source: authors

Interior partition walls are on wooden frames covered by plasterboard. Where this has been smashed, traces of the original light and dark blue painted walls are visible. All the floors have suspended ceilings and visible air-conditioning ducts. An earlier visitor to the building reported the presence of thick wire ethernet transceivers and shielded cables (http://dasalte. ccc.de/teufelsberg). The first floor is divided into three rooms. Adjacent to the stairs is a self-contained room with a serving hatch on its north wall. The upper floor is divided into two open rooms and against the eastern wall is a small closet. On all floors the frequency of electrical sockets around the walls suggests the former presence of computer equipment. At the northern end of the western side each floor is served by double external doors which were used for the installation of equipment.

Beyond the stairs to [1437A] in the corridor's north wall is a set of double doors to an electrical switch room [1468B] with metal cabinets to either side. At this point the east to west corridor turns through a right-angle southwards towards the British building [1455]. On its east side before reaching this building is a red door to the incinerator room [1455B]. Internally, a large orange incinerator dominates the room. Information on its control panel records it as a 'Pyrorolyseanlage, Compactronia CE150' manufactured by Cornel Schmidt of Leverhusen in 1984. Just beyond this room a set of glass doors in a red metal frame mark the entrance to the British building [1455].

1469 Document destruction building

Returning to the main corridor, to the west it leads to the document destruction building [1469] that was added during the 1978–1982 building campaign. It is sturdily built, with solid brick walls laid to English bond with a flat concrete roof (Figure 5.19). Internally, it is divided into two uneven parts: the taller northern section is about 12m tall and the

Figure 5.19 1469. To the right is the document destruction building [1469] with an external loading bay. To the rear is a door to the main corridor that probably gave access to the GCHQ mast base close to the bush in the mid ground. Just visible to the rear of the bush are the burnt-out remains of steel containers that were used as a gymnasium

Source: authors

Figure 5.20 1469. Paper shredding machine manufactured by Document Disintegration Systems, LLF Industries, Huntingdon Park, California
Source: authors

southern section somewhat lower. A single internal door connects the two rooms. From the corridor the building is entered through double doors in the north wall. This opens into the southern room where there are two paper shredders by 'Document Disintegration Systems, LLF Industries, Huntingdon Park, California' and a number of electrical switch cabinets (Figure 5.20).

After shredding, the paper was fed through two pipes in the partition wall to the top of two hoppers. These in turn fed into pulping machines and finally the shredded and pulped paper was passed into a hydraulic press where it was formed into blocks (Figure 5.21). On the north side of the building is a double door with a loading bay and set of steps sheltered by a concrete canopy. From here the shredded and pulped paper was removed for final disposal.

Dust samples were taken from the shredders and found to contain a mass of fibres and black flecks, which may be carbon paper. The results are unsurprising given that a massive amount of paper came through this room to be pulped and shredded before being taken off site to be burnt. They are however reassuring in the way the purpose of the site is reflected in the scientific samples recovered (Figure 5.22).

Figure 5.21 1469. Bale-making machines. Shredded paper was delivered through the rear pipe to the hopper and then into the pulping and bale-making machine

Source: Angus Boulton

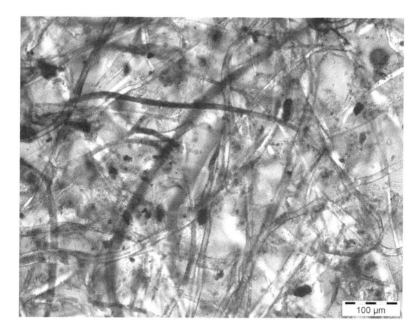

Figure 5.22 1469. Mass of paper fibre and black flecks which may be the remains of carbon copy paper. The sample was taken from the bottom of shredder

Source: Yasmin Shand

1498 Bar

During the early 1980s an L-shaped building was inserted to the east of the document destruction building [1469] and between the arms of the main corridor [1460]. To the west the building may be entered from the northern access road through a set of double external doors that gives access to a central corridor. On entering, to the west is a metal cage and to its rear a rectangular storeroom with two doors. The guard units probably used these and the cages may have been used as dog kennels. Along the eastern side of the corridor are six small rooms: the rear four were stores, while two to the north also provide access to a large open room to the east. This large room with a herringbone-pattern brick floor was probably used as a rest area (Figure 5.23).

The three inner walls were lined in wooden boards and the roof is supported on wooden columns to give the impression of a traditional German bier-keller. Since abandonment, this room has been seriously fire

Figure 5.23 1498, Bar. To the right was an enclosed garden. The steps led up to the main internal corridor

Source: authors

damaged. Its south wall was half glazed and overlooked an open courtyard to the south that was probably used as a seating area. In its southeast corner a set of steps leads up to the corridor [1460]. Close to their base is a concrete tethering block for the British antenna mast that was sited to the north.

Immediately to the north of this area is a corridor whose primary function appears to have been to provide access to the British mast. This was a 120m-tall, red and white antenna manufactured by Rohde and Schwarz in the early 1970s at a cost of around 3 million Deutschmarks (TNA: FO 1060/5536, 31 August 1976). It is believed to have been a GCHQ facility. A circular, red steel mounting plate marks its position, and radiating from it are six heavy concrete tethering blocks that were used to secure the mast (Figure 5.24). One of these blocks was, as previously described, within the outdoor seating area adjacent to [1498].

To the north of the corridor, and to provide accommodation for a gymnasium, four metal shipping containers were added into the angle created by this and the main north-to-south corridor. They too have been seriously fire damaged.

Figure 5.24 Base of the British General Communications Head Quarters' (GCHQ) mast

Source: authors

1425 The Arctic Tower

Returning to the western arm of the main corridor, at its western end is the Arctic Tower [1425], one of the oldest buildings on the site and probably completed about 1965 (Figure 5.25). This is a 12-sided, three-storey, steel-framed structure clad in windowless ribbed aluminium sheeting and topped by a radome about 16m in diameter.

The Arctic Tower is entered from the main corridor [1460] on its south side via a secondary projecting stair turret with a central lift shaft. This gives access to the two workrooms (Figure 5.26) while a door from the second floor leads to a ladder and hinged access hatch to the asphalt-covered roof. At its centre is a hexagonal steel-girder mounting for a rotating surveillance device (Figure 5.27). Set into the roof are cable conduits that carried data to the lower monitoring rooms. Internally, the first-floor and second-floor rooms are lined with pressed steel sheets, and both have suspended linoleum-covered floors and suspended ceilings with recessed lighting. On each floor are work bays around the exterior walls, probably for analysts or radar operators. Floor plugs and wall-mounted cable conduits indicate the presence of computer cabinets.

Figure 5.25 1425, The Arctic Tower from [1456]. In the foreground is the brick
Document Destruction Building [1469]

Source: authors

Figure 5.26 1425, The Arctic Tower. Interior showing the individual work positions. The door to the rear leads to the staircase

Source: authors

Figure 5.27 1425, The Arctic Tower, antenna base. To the right is the hatch that gives access into this area

Source: authors

1465 Jambalaya tower

To the southwest is the latest tower on the site [1465], constructed about 1989 (Figure 5.28). It sits on the site of an earlier and unidentified listening device that was probably installed during the late 1970s (Bowman 1997, Figure 3.6). Tower [1465], also known as Jambalaya, comprises a three-storey circular brick tower surmounted by a radome. It is entered through a single door on its east side and above this is a door and wooden balcony

Figure 5.28 1465, Jambalaya tower, constructed about 1989

Source: authors

at second floor level. Externally, below the top of the tower, is a galvanised steel walkway that provides access around the base of the dome. From the balcony a ladder gave access to a hatch on its south side, which is close to a square opening in the radome. To the north of the balcony are metal fixings that previously held a vertical ladder.

1455 The British building, Building M

As described above, from the main corridor a set of red doors connected to the British, or RAF, building [1455] (Figure 5.29). This was principally occupied by personnel from the RAF's 26 Signals Unit, but also included staff from the army's Intelligence Corps and civilians from the Government Communications Headquarters (GCHQ). A small number of RAF police controlled access to the building. Employees of the British Civil Service Property Services Agency (PSA) carried out maintenance work in the building. Personnel working in the building included listening specialists, cryptographers and translators (Beckmann et al. 2011, 106). The different organisations had differing intelligence objectives. The RAF and Army targeted their Warsaw Pact equivalents, while GCHQ had wider

Figure 5.29 1455, outer doors to the British Building M. To the left the red door is the entry to the incinerator room 1455B

Source: authors

interests including political intelligence on Eastern Europe. A veteran recalls that the RAF occupied the upper floor and the army the ground floor, which may imply that from late 1982 GCHQ personnel were located in the adjacent building [1475]. Within all areas the multitude of rooms and interconnections between them reflect the compartmentalisation of workflows (Figures 5.30 and 5.31).

Building 1455 is a double-storey building partly terraced into the hill. The lower storey has reinforced concrete walls and the upper storey is steel-framed with block work infill. It was built during the major Filman construction project between 1969 and 1972. An aerial photograph confirms that the building was externally complete by July 1971 (Figure 3.7). As originally completed, it was a rectangular, windowless building with three open emergency staircases on its south side. It measures about 52m x 27m

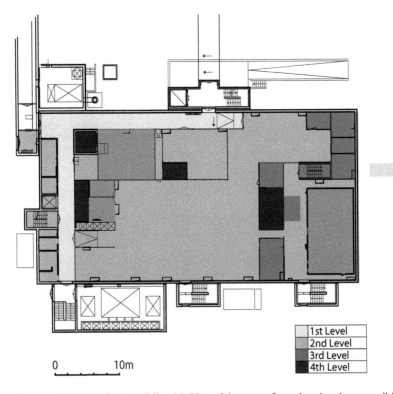

1st Level
2nd Level
3rd Level
4th Level

0   10m

Figure 5.30 1455, RAF Building M. Plan of the upper floor showing the accessibility of different areas

Source: Redrawn from plan provided by Berlin Technical University on Field Station Berlin by Katharina Beckmann, David Derksen, Robert Haesecke-Diesing and Florian Leitner

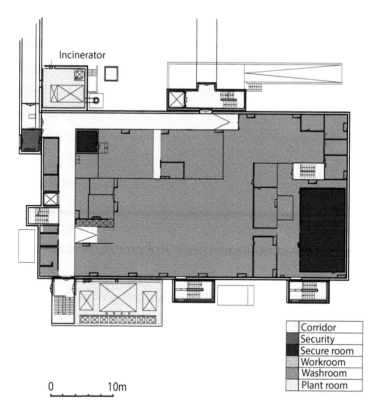

Figure 5.31 1455, RAF Building M. Plan of the upper floor showing the rooms characterised by function

Source: Redrawn from plan provided by Berlin Technical University on Field Station Berlin by Katharina Beckmann, David Derksen, Robert Haesecke-Diesing and Florian Leitner

and stands about 10m tall. There is a further enclosed staircase on its west side, which also gave access to the roof. During the later 1970s, computing technology underwent a rapid evolution, when smaller and cheaper digital systems were able to compete with the earlier mainframe machines. Evidence suggests that the building was refurbished on at least one occasion around 1980, a change perhaps both prompted by technological developments and the era's increase in defence expenditure. On the south wall some of the most visible changes around this date included the demolition of the western emergency staircase and the addition of the plant room [1455A]. The other two emergency staircases were enclosed and on the north side a first floor link was constructed to the new building [1475].

As described above, all personnel entered the complex through the Guardroom [1454] and along the main corridor [1460] to the northwest corner of building [1455]. This led to a set of red metal-framed doors facing a further guardroom which controlled access through another set of doors to the upper corridor of the building (Figure 5.32).

These doors were interconnected and effectively created a holding area where no more than three or four people would be admitted for checking (Manton 2015, 129). Inside this inner guardroom was a large electrical switch-board. The covered corridor was completed a year or two after this building, so this may represent the original personnel entrance to the building. In the north wall is another entrance with an external ramp that was used for moving technical deliveries, and a later lift shaft and stairs for access to the upper British floor of building [1475].

Having passed through at least three security checks, once inside the building movement was fairly open. On entering from the inner guardroom there is an L-shaped corridor along the north and west sides of the building, covered in a dimpled black vinyl surface. The northern corridor is adjacent to the wall and gives access to the rear doors. On its north wall is an electrical switch box. On the opposite side of the corridor were metal panel walls

Figure 5.32 1455, inner door to the British Building M. To the left is the doorway
to the RAF police guardroom

Source: authors

with high windows that screened activities within the main computer processing rooms. Along the western side of the west corridor, which is painted light blue, are two probable storerooms, a lift, the staircase leading to the roof and ground floor (Figure 5.33), another small room of uncertain use and in the southwest corner male and female toilets. The main operational area occupied the remainder of the floor. This could be entered at three points:

Figure 5.33 1455, RAF Building M. West staircase at the ground floor level

from the north corridor through a single door, through double doors with a ramp at its east end or through double doors, again with a ramp, off the western corridor.

Heat was an unwanted by-product of the enormous computer processing power of the Teufelsberg. In the computer suites a universal feature was the use of raised floors to house cable conduits and air-conditioning ducts, above which were suspended ceilings concealing further air-conditioning equipment (Figure 5.34). In common with the other computer processing areas, these were mounted on suspended access floors and to enter this area from the corridor were either steps or ramps, essential for wheeling computer equipment in and out of these areas. The floors are supported on adjustable metal pedestal legs that in turn supported a metal framework that held heavy, square, calcium sulphate, metal-backed floor panels, usually covered in blue carpet which could be lifted to gain access to the under-floor void. Beneath the suspended floor the concrete floor slab is surfaced with vinyl tiles, which may represent the original floor surface. Makers' marks on some of the slabs confirmed they were standard commercial products supplied by Mero of Prichsenstadt, Bavaria. Most of the internal partition

Figure 5.34 1455, RAF Building M. Ground floor showing the suspended floor, air-conditioning vent and frames for partition walls

Source: authors

walls are prefabricated metal panels, a system that permitted the floor to be relatively easily reconfigured to new requirements. Another feature of this area are vertical ventilation ducts arranged around the external walls and on some of the internal partitions. These were used to cool the computer cabinets. Above was a suspended ceiling of square, pressed-metal panels backed with insulation foam. This concealed air-conditioning ducts and cable conduits.

Wrapped around the northeast corner of this floor are four fairly small rooms, each entered through a single door. The walls of these rooms are covered in sound insulating boards, which may suggest that they housed noisy machines, such as telex, or other types of tape printers. Next to the southern one of these rooms is a staircase leading to the ground floor. In the southeast corner is a large, freestanding galvanised steel metal room with panelled interior and exterior walls. This arrangement created a 'Faraday cage', a feature that prevented the escape of electronic emissions and might also be used to create a secure conference room. To its west are four self-contained rooms, with a blank wall facing the large open central area. The northern three appear to have been entered through a single door, while the southern one is freestanding and also entered through a single door. These gave additional privacy and might have been used by the commanding officer. In its latest phase the voice operators, tasked with listening to Warsaw Pact spoken communications, occupied the large central area. Each was allocated a booth-like workstation. On the northern side of this area are two large rooms and a single smaller room, created from panels, with large internal windows. The shift supervisors probably occupied these rooms.

In the northwest corner of this area is a small, secure room with solid concrete walls. To enter this from the adjacent office involves stepping down to a single steel door in its east wall. At floor level are pipe conduits for heavy-duty power cables and data cable bundles (Figure 5.35). These pipes, and others in the building, may have been pressurised to prevent attempts to tap the wires. Another distinctive security feature of this room was its copper lining, traces of which survive around the base of the walls and where cable plates penetrated the walls (Figure 5.36). In its eastern wall is a window covered by a metal mesh screen to complete the circuit of the Faraday cage. To its south are four small rooms divided by metal panel walls, the southerly three of which were occupied by the counter-intelligence team.

As described above, the ground floor could be accessed from the lift or staircases on the west corridor and within the main operational area. In common with the upper floor there is an L-shaped corridor, although the north corridor is set back from the exterior wall. In the southwest corner are male and female toilets and to the north of the lift are stores, the central one with a sliding door, while the one to its north is tile lined. In the northwest corner

Figure 5.35 1455, RAF Building M, Room 55.016. Possibly pressurised cables passing into a secure room. Note also the wire mesh window to complete the circuit of the Faraday cage

Source: authors

Figure 5.36 1455, RAF Building M, Room 55.016. Remains of copper cladding around a cable plate

Source: authors

of this floor is a sound-proof room with a single door and a cable panel in its east wall. Along the north wall, whose exterior is partly set into the mound, are three secure rooms. To the west is a large room formed of breeze blocks. Externally, it is covered by lower smooth panels above, which are square-pressed metal sound-absorbing panels. It is entered through a door in its east wall, adjacent to which is a small window with a serving hatch below that allowed documents and other small items to be deposited and issued. Adjacent to this was a pipe that may have been pressurised to maintain its security. This window and another one to the north have an imbedded wire mesh to maintain the electrical conductivity of the room's lining. Internally, it has been thoroughly stripped, although the hangers for the suspended ceiling remain with some air-conditioning conduits. In its west wall is a cable panel connecting to the sound-proof room in the northwest corner. Around the cable panel is a piece of copper, indicating that this room was also a copper-lined Faraday cage. Also hanging from the cable panel was a Radio Frequency Interference Filter, manufactured by Belling and Lee, Ltd of Enfield, Middlesex (Figure 5.37).

At the northern end of the east wall another door gave access to an office and a small square vault with solid walls and a single door. A steel security door with substantial pins that entered into its frame originally protected this

Figure 5.37 1455, RAF Building M. Radio Frequency Interference Filter, manufactured by Belling and Lee, Ltd of Enfield, Middlesex

Source: authors

room (https://web.archive.org/web/20100224072114/http://dasalte.ccc.de/teufelsberg/ 11-2-19). Although the door has been removed, the holes in the frame remain. This room was also lined with smooth lower panels and upper pressed-metal sound-absorbing panels above. Adjacent to this was another office that could be accessed from this room and the main corridor. In the northeast corner of the building is another large Faraday cage. This comprises a freestanding box formed from bolted steel sheets with a narrow gap between it and the exterior wall of the building (Figure 5.38). Internally, it is divided into two rooms. A smaller room at its east end is entered through a single door. Entry into the second room was from a single door at its west end that was monitored from a small window set into the wall, originally secured by a pneumatic lock. The rooms have suspended floors and ceilings, and were lined in wooden panelling. This higher standard of wall finish may indicate that they were used as secure meeting and conference rooms.

The remainder of the building comprises a rectangular block of rooms to the southeast. To the west is a block of seven rooms surrounded by solid block walls, except for a cut-out in the northwest corner which has two panel walls on the corridor side. To the southwest and opposite the toilets a ramp leads up to the communal kitchen that served both floors. On its west wall is a range of fitted kitchen units and above these are mushroom-coloured

Figure 5.38 1455, RAF Building M. This room was composed of metal panels to create a Faraday cage and was probably used for meetings, ensuring that they were secure from Warsaw Pact counter-surveillance

Source: authors

tiles that overlie an orange painted wall. Adjacent to the kitchen units the area has a cork floor while the remainder is covered in blue carpet. To the north of the kitchen, and also entered up a ramp is a suite of three rooms. On the doors to this area is a sticker ('PSA Berlin') referring to the Property Services Agency which, until the 1990s, was the British government's estate management organisation. On the rear of the door is a Union Jack sticker. The two main rooms in this area are surfaced with cork floor tiles and the west wall is covered by sound insulation boards. To the northeast is a step down to a secure store with an external wire cage wall, and its other walls are lined with pressed-metal sound-absorbing panels. In the northwest corner is a self-contained office entered from the corridor, and adjacent to this is a telecommunications exchange room with a single door from the corridor. The room in the southeast corner of this block could only be accessed from the eastern main operations area.

This eastern main operating area was divided into ten rooms. Two of the rooms were accessed from the main northern corridor, but due to the demolition of the wall panels defining these rooms it is unclear if they also connected with the rooms to the south. At the eastern end of the northern corridor is the staircase to the upper floor, and immediately before the stairs a pair of double doors leads into a suite of three offices. Again it is uncertain if these were linked to the two large rooms to the west. These rooms dominated the ground floor and former personnel recall that they housed army voice operators with shift supervisors in the surrounding offices. From the northern corridor entry into these rooms was up a ramp and through a set of double doors. This area has a suspended floor with heavy, square concrete blocks covered with blue carpet supported on a metal framework on linoleum tiles. Above, air-conditioning conduits were concealed behind a suspended ceiling. In the southeast corner of the ground floor is a smaller rectangular secure room with solid concrete walls. This has been thoroughly stripped and offers no clues to its function. To the southwest is a self-contained office defined by metal panel walls and a separate door to another self-contained office in the western block of rooms. Air conditioning around this area was through vertical metal ducts, most of which were arranged around the exterior walls, although there were a number in the central area. In common with the upper floor, the ground floor was probably refitted at least once. The rooms with solid walls and without suspended floors may represent part of the original configuration of the building.

In the early 1980s, a new air-conditioning plant [1455A] was added to the south side of the building, replacing the western stair tower. It is a two-storey reinforced concrete structure that abuts the original building. Probably due to the unstable ground beneath, it is slowly separating from the main building. At its west side a new internal staircase was built, while air-conditioning fans took up most of the building; Wilhelm Gebardt GmbH of Waldenburg supplied those on the top floor. It was probably also at this time that the other two staircases were enclosed. The construction of the new external plant room during the 1980s raises the question of where the original plant room was located. On a 1971 air photograph (Figure 3.7) between the western and central external staircases there are at least two grills on the wall, which may be air intakes. To their rear is the group of rooms defined by solid walls that may delineate the position of the original plant room.

Access to the roof is from the staircase on the western side of the building. Asphalt sheeting covers the roof and steel railings protect its edge, with mountings for surveillance cameras on its corners. On the roof-level landing is a separate room that houses a hydraulic pump supplied by Ziehl-Abbeg of Kuenzelsau. A plate confirms it was manufactured during the 1970s, although the last digit is illegible. A door gives access onto the roof where there are six supports for vertical antennae (Figures 5.39 and 5.40).

These were supported by two steel pipes on top of which was a hinge mechanism that allowed the masts to be raised to the vertical by a hand winch set between the posts. The firm Gedi supplied these in 1970. Linking the mast supports are lines of pierced steel conduits supported on low concrete blocks, which carried cabling between the masts. On the south side of the building is a crane that was used to lift equipment onto the roof. A plate on the crane confirms that it was also installed in 1970. In the southeast corner of the roof are two horizontal girders that may have supported a steel gantry with further listening devices.

Also as part of the 1980s alterations, a new access building was constructed on the north side of the building. As described above, the building [1455] is partly set into the side of the mound, and to bring the new entry into the building at first floor level a ramp was constructed from the east giving access to a set of double doors. These gave access to the first floor and, within the annex, to a set of stairs to the east and lift shaft to the west. This annex projects above roof level and from it personnel from the British building could pass to the upper British floor of the new building [1475] by means of a covered bridge. This too has a suspended floor with data conduits beneath.

Externally, at the southeast corner of the British building [1455] is a square concrete base 5.9m wide set slightly off-square to the main structure (Figures 5.41 and 5.42). At each corner are concrete columns 97cm high, with 36cm square metal mounting plates that supported a gantry for two parabolic dishes (Bowman 1997, Figure 3.6). This may represent the DSS facility that was completed by November 1980 (TNA: AIR/28/2215 November 1980).

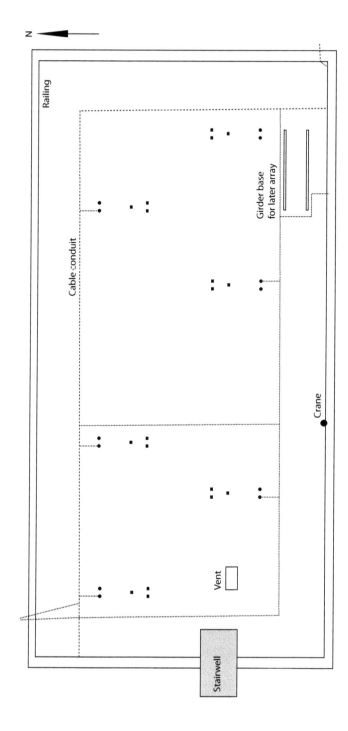

Figure 5.39 1455, RAF Building M, roof plan

Source: authors

Figure 5.40 1455, RAF Building M. Roof, slowing the antennae supports and cable channels

Source: authors

Figure 5.41 1455, RAF Building M, southeast corner. These footings may be the remains of the DSS Installation, which was installed in about 1980

Source: Angus Boulton

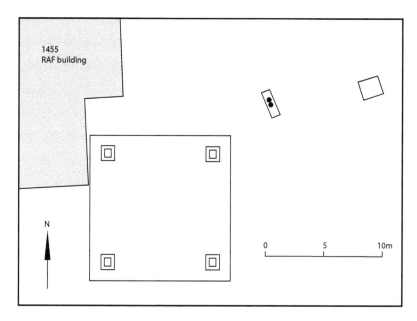

Figure 5.42 1455, RAF Building M. Plan of footings for the possible DSS Installation

Source: authors

To the north, outside the building, in a 'courtyard' created by the various buildings around it, is a basketball net on the concrete surface, presumably installed by the Americans for use during breaks. At a site where functionality and secrecy are key, signs of leisure activities introduce a social strand to the otherwise dominant military and political narratives.

1475 Teufelsberg II, Building U

During the late 1970s and early 1980s as part of an expansion and refurbishment programme, the capacity of the station was greatly increased by the commissioning of building [1475] in late 1982 (Figure 5.43). This is a massive, two-storey, steel-framed building, infilled with breeze blocks and clad externally in blue cement sheets supported on a metal framework with rock wool insulation (Figure 5.44); in common with most other buildings on the site, it is windowless.

The main part of the building measures 42m x 38m and stands about 13m tall. To the west is a smaller annex about 35m x 15m. British and American

Figure 5.43 1475, Teufelsberg II. In the foreground is the staircase tower between the US ground floor and British upper floor. On the roof is a foundation for a radome that was never installed

Source: authors

Figure 5.44 1475, Teufelsberg II. Detail of external cladding to the Teufelsberg II

Source: authors

personnel occupied the building, and although it appears to have been speci-fied as one building project, its layout reflects the lack of day-to-day contact between the two countries, a regime where each ran their own operations. Most of the rooms have suspended floors with cable conduits beneath and suspended ceilings of perforated pressed-metal panels, with a large void above for air-conditioning ducts. Fluorescent light units set into the ceilings lit the rooms. Most of the metal fittings in the building, including steel doors and handrails, are painted brown, a colour that was common on many 1980s United States installations. On the roof of the building is a low, circular concrete foundation for a radome. It was apparently unused (Figure 5.43).

The upper British floor

As described above, access for British personnel was across a covered bridge at first floor level on the north side of the British building [1455]. This led to a lobby with double doors to either side. The layout of the rooms suggests that originally a corridor ran the full width of the building to a staircase on the north side. Returning to the entrance lobby, to the left, double doors give access to an L-shaped corridor, and on its south side a large cable bundle passed through the exterior wall to a cable conduit on the outside of the build-ing. The corridor is set on a suspended floor with a central blue carpet strip with brown carpet along the walls.

Along the western side of the building are five rooms. The southernmost four rooms operated as a single unit. In the southwest corner is a vault or magazine with solid walls and two steel vault doors. On the eastern door is the remains of a Ministry of Defence notice, a sentence of which reads 'A copy of this poster is to be displayed conspicuously at each explosives area and at each entrance to every magazine, explosives storehouses . . .'. This suite of rooms was entered through a split door in the room to the north of the secure rooms, and the room to its north also had a door from the main corridor. The fourth office was entered through an internal door. It is possible that this suite of rooms fulfilled a similar function to the armoury within the main United States' building [1458], and may have contained small arms and other emergency equipment, including explosive demolition charges. To the north of this room is a larger rectangular room with a single door from the corridor. Internally, it has a suspended floor covered in cork tiles and in its southeast corner are a number of circular holes which probably carried data cables from below the floor to cabinets within the room (Figure 5.45). Returning to the corridor, on its west wall is a switch cup-board and beyond are doors leading to a lobby and internal staircase.

At some point the suggested original north-to-south axial corridor was blocked and divided into two rooms; the northern one about double the length of the southern one (Figure 5.46). The southern room may be entered

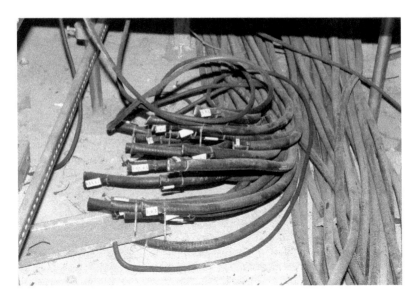

Figure 5.45 1475, Teufelsberg II. First floor, Room 75.1.53, typical of cable bundles found beneath many floors

Source: authors

Figure 5.46 1475, Teufelsberg II, Room 75.1.29. Possible original axial corridor later divided into rooms, looking north

Source: authors

from a door to the east and in turn another door provides access to the northern room, which also has a single door in its northern wall connecting to the lobby area. The floor of the northern room is covered in cork squares, which may suggest it contained computing equipment.

This former corridor and the main western corridor define a rectangular block of nine offices, all of which are accessed from the western corridor. To the south, immediately adjacent to the double corridor doors, is a door into a single self-contained room. Turning the corner, a single door in the east wall leads to a suite of four rooms. To the north of these are a further four self-contained rooms all entered through single doors from the corridor.

Returning to the main entrance, the eastern corridor is dog-legged and gives access to a large suite of rooms in the north-eastern part of the building: three rooms to the north and in the southeast corner of the building a group of four offices. Three of these are self-contained offices entered from single doors off the corridor, all of which have traces of wood-effect panelling. The fourth, and larger, room to the east is well-equipped with wall sockets, suggesting the presence of computing equipment. Off the main corridor, a T-shaped corridor connects to a door to the now demolished eastern plant rooms. On the northern side of the dog-legged corridor are three rooms, all entered from the corridor. The eastern two rooms are linked by an internal door.

In the northeast corner of the building is a large group of 11 interconnected rooms which operated as a single functional unit. These rooms were entered from the dog-leg corridor to the south and also from the northern lobby through a vestibule with doors to either side; to the southeast there is also a single door to the T-shaped corridor. At the heart of this group is a large open room; to its west are four rooms, entered through single doors. The room in the southwest corner is windowless and may indicate a particularly sensitive function. To the east, three doors provide access to large open rooms to the south and north, separated from one another by a narrow room entered from a smaller lobby area (Figures 5.47 and 5.48).

This may indicate the position of a more highly restricted computer, or possibly the officer in charge of this section. To the south of the larger southern room are two further offices, divided internally by a sliding door. Prefabricated aluminium panels with double-glazed upper sections divide the area. This prevented conversations being overheard, while allowing activities within the rooms to be overseen.

Against the north wall of the building is a large room entered through two single doors from the western corridor. To the east and from the northern lobby a steel door gives access to an external stair turret and to the west to a room with evidence for fire suppressant halon gas bottles. In

Figure 5.47 1475, Teufelsberg II, first floor room 75.1.32 looking north
Source: authors

Figure 5.48 1475, Teufelsberg II, first floor Room 75.1.32. Typical suspended ceiling with air-conditioning plant
Source: authors

the northwest corner of the building there is an internal staircase leading up from the northern, ground floor entrance lobby, opening at the top to a single narrow door. To the east of the staircase is a self-contained room of unknown function. The staircase door opens out onto a lobby with a solid terrazzo floor (Figure 5.49).

To the east a set of double doors lead to the western access corridor and to the west a single door leads to lavatories, washrooms and briefing rooms. On the south wall of the lobby a shallow recess marks the position of the void of the unused lift shaft. This was clearly an integral part of the original design of the building. It may indicate that during the construction of the building its role was altered and may be linked to the decision not to install a radome on its roof (Figure 5.43). By omitting the lift, direct access between the American ground floor and British upper floor was restricted to a single staircase and door (see below and Figures 5.52 and 5.53).

Figure 5.49 1475, Teufelsberg II, lobby area of the northwest corner of the first floor. Double doors from the western corridor open out into the lobby. Beyond, a single door leads to washrooms, a small kitchen and briefing rooms. Also note the high-quality finish given to the interior walls

Source: authors

To the east is the narrower rectangular annex. From the lobby there is an L-shaped corridor leading to an external staircase turret on the south wall, which leads directly to the outer yard with no connection to the ground floor. To the south, in the angle of the 'L', are male and female lavatories and washrooms, and storerooms. On the northern side of the corridor there is a narrow kitchenette, with brown tiled walls and a cork floor that was previously equipped with fitted kitchen units. To its west are two briefing rooms entered through single doors (Figure 5.50).

On the south wall of the eastern and larger room are remains of a screen or display board. Separating the two rooms was a Perspex screen that allowed people in the smaller western room to view the presentation while preserving their anonymity. At the end of the corridor were the most secure rooms on this level. A steel door, originally secured with a combination lock, protected this area (Figure 5.51). This gave access to a lobby with doors to rooms to the north and south, and to the west was another steel door also previously secured with a combination lock. This opened out into two large rooms with suspended floors separated by a glazed panel wall with sliding door between the two.

Figure 5.50 1475, Teufelsberg II, first floor briefing room 75.1.21. The hole in the wall was originally filled by a one-way screen. Out of view to the left was a projection screen

Source: authors

Figure 5.51 1475, Teufelsberg II, first floor. Combination lock cover of the secure
door protecting access to the eastern rooms

Source: authors

The lower United States floor

United States personnel entered the lower floor of the building from the
main corridor [1460] that turns around the northwest corner of the building's
western annex. In the northwest corner of the main building is a lobby with
a solid artificial stone terrazzo floor. To the west is the staircase to the first
floor (Figures 5.52 and 5.53).

Also to the west is a single door to the annex and to the east a set of
double doors leading to ground floor rooms. On the rear wall a recess in
the wall marks the position of the unused lift entrance (Figure 5.54). This
has recently been breached and confirms the existence of the unfinished lift
shaft. On the eastern side of the lobby is a series of electrical switchgear
cabinets. The ground floor rooms could also be accessed from a single door
in the south wall, although its outward opening may indicate a fire escape.
There is also a wide opening in the eastern wall, which previously connected
to the demolished plant rooms.

Figure 5.52 1475, Teufelsberg II, ground floor. North side of the building, main lobby entrance – the staircase leads to the upper British floor

Source: authors

Figure 5.53 1475, Teufelsberg II, first floor. Single door entry on to the upper British floor

Source: authors

Figure 5.54 1475, Teufelsberg II, ground floor. North side of the building main lobby entrance – sealed lift shaft with a recent attempt to break into the void

Source: authors

To the west, the double doors open into a linoleum-lined corridor. To the north is a self-contained switch room, and to its north a self-contained room with a single door to the main corridor. On the western side of the corridor is a room adjacent to the lift shaft, which may have contained electrical switchgear and corresponds to the equivalent room above. This corridor also gives access to four self-contained rooms in the southwest corner of the building. A large open work area with linoleum-covered floor slabs dominates the eastern part of the building. This is accessed from the corridor through a double set of doors. Above this is the painted notice, 'Maintenance Building'. As will be discussed below, the building has been used as a film set and it is possible that this is a later addition. Along the north wall is a suite of four rooms accessed from a single door off the central room. This room has a suspended floor with linoleum-covered floor slabs. Above is a deep suspended ceiling with large air-conditioning ducts, further cable conduits and large suspended electrical junction boxes. On the eastern external wall are a number of ventilation duct openings and a scar marking the position of the demolished plant room annex.

As described above, to the northwest is a suite of four interconnected rooms, and to their east are two other self-contained rooms also entered from the central area. To the east is a large room originally floored in linoleum-covered floor slabs, with a small square room in its southwest corner with a cork floor. Its eastern wall is lined in wood-effect panels (Figure 5.55). Due to later modifications by a film company, it is unclear where the original doors to this area were. In the southeast corner of this floor are an enclosed switch room and a kitchen area lined in brown tiles with a solid tile floor and two cooker hoods. To its west is a large room that may have acted as a dining area and to its north two rooms entered from the central area. In the southwest corner of the building is a further group of seven rooms, but demolition of most of the dividing walls has obscured the relationships between them.

The interpretation of this floor has been complicated by its later use as a film or TV set. As described above, it is uncertain whether or not the painted 'Maintenance Building' sign in the access corridor is original or part of the set. It's now grey painted walls may also result from its use as a film set. However it is the large room to the east that appears to have undergone the most modification. Grey painted wooden sheeting has covered the walls of the central room (Figure 5.56). To the north is a set of split, stable type

Figure 5.55 1475, Teufelsberg II, ground floor, eastern room 75.0.35. This shows a typical 1980s room with deep suspended floors and ceilings and wood-effect wall panels

Source: authors

Figure 5.56 1475, Teufelsberg II, ground floor, Room 75.0.32. The appearance of this room has been considerably altered for film work by covering the original walls, repainting and inserting false walls

Source: authors

doors, but it is unclear whether these are original or an addition by the film company. To their south a wooden sliding door has been fabricated, which was operated from the rear by pulling a rope. A jagged hole in the door simulates a missile strike. The outer walls of the large eastern room were covered in grey cloth secured on wooden batons and around the outer edges are a block board surface delimited by yellow and black hazard tape, presumably to create a smooth surface for the camera trollies. A short section of this trolley floor also survives to the west of the kitchen.

As described above, the western annex may be entered from a single door off the main ground floor lobby; four of its rooms could also be entered from the main corridor [1460]. In the southeast corner of the annex are male and female toilets, washrooms and stores arranged in an identical configuration to those on the upper floor. To the north of the internal corridor is a suite of nine interconnected rooms. Internally these are entered through a single door, and two of the rooms may also be accessed from the main outer corridor. All these rooms have cork-finished floor slabs and most of the rooms have prefabricated, white aluminium panel plain walls, with the exception of a room against the outer corridor. This has a single wooden panel wall and also a row of wall sockets. The presence of a halon fire suppressant system in this room indicates the former presence of a computer. At its western end the corridor gives access to two large rooms, both of which may also be entered from the main external corridor. In the southeast corner of the eastern room is a small office with a window in its west side, and in its southwest corner is an air filtration unit connected to below-floor conduits. Both of these rooms have cork floors and the west wall of the easternmost room is lined in wooden panelling as is the western room. It has been suggested that these rooms were used for the training of American linguists and translators (Beckmann et al. 2011, 106).

1458 Main operations building

Dominating the site is the three-storey main operations building [1458], with its tower and three distinctive radomes (Figure 5.57). In the late 1990s, this building was identified for retention and conversion into apartments. It was to

Figure 5.57 1458, main operations building with three radomes. In the foreground is the western end of Teufelsberg II [1475]

Source: Angus Boulton

be stripped back to its frame and its blank exterior walls replaced with windows to give stunning views across the city. Although this scheme was abandoned, most of the preparatory demolition work was carried out and in so doing has removed most of the evidence for the former configuration of this building. It is suggested that there were three broad activities carried out in the building: on the upper floor, signals collection; analysis on the middle floor; and on the ground floor, onward transmission of data (Beckmann et al. 2011, 102).

The building dates from the major 1969–1972 construction programme. It measures about 61m x 23m and is supported on a massive steel framework with solid concrete floors and roof. Internally, it is divided into 11 bays with an off-centre line of columns. This design was adopted to accommodate the base of the central tower and to provide space for a longitudinal corridor. To ensure the frame's rigidity, it is cross-braced around it outer edges. Each of the floors appears abnormally tall, about 5.5m, a feature designed to house suspended floors and deep suspended ceilings, behind which were cable conduits and air-conditioning ducting (Figure 5.58).

Figure 5.58 1458, Room 58.0.21. Ground floor showing the massive steel frame and the deep floor and ceiling voids and the wooden room panelling

Source: authors

Along its longitudinal sides the outer steel columns project and the outer wall is a non-load-bearing concrete frame infilled with concrete blocks (Figure 5.59). This and the projecting columns were clad in blue cement sheets supported on a metal framework with rock wool insulation. Three white horizontal bands and the vertical columns that were also covered by white panels

Figure 5.59 1458, northeast wall and central lift tower

Source: authors

reinforced the geometric form of this building. Projecting from either end of the building were concrete emergency staircases. The one to the east has been demolished. On the south side of the building is a projecting technical annex. This is slightly shorter than the main building rising to about two and a half storeys. Above the roof is a narrower projection that continues to roof level to connect with the ducts above the upper ceiling. This annex was independent of the main building and entered from a door on its west side, which gave access to a flight of stairs. Internally were fans and large air-conditioning ducts.

For most personnel, entry into the building was along the main covered corridor [1460] that took them to an entrance on the south side of the building. Just before the entry doors, a door to the east gave access to the electrical switch room [1467]. On the north side of the building was a set of double outward-opening doors, but these were probably only used for the delivery of equipment and other goods. There were also single doors on the north side of the building and in its two end walls. All of these were probably only for emergency use. The southern entrance from the corridor into the building led into a large lobby area and then through a set of double doors into another lobby area. To the rear is the square concrete base of the central tower. At the centre of this is a square lift (elevator) shaft surrounded by an external staircase. On each floor this was entered through double doors in a steel framework with upper sections glazed in bullet-proof glass (Figure 5.60).

Figure 5.60 1458, first floor central lift shaft
Source: authors

Also on each floor at the rear of the lift shaft were lavatories and shower rooms. On the ground floor, to the west of the lift, were two technical equipment rooms and to the east three rooms, the entrance from the lobby area being protected by a steel cage type door. This gave access to an armoury and emergency stores including gas masks (Beckmann et al. 2011, 102). These rooms could be entered from another room to the east, with a door from the main corridor giving access to a serving hatch, which was probably used to issue arms and equipment. Curiously, in the eastern wall of the room with the serving hatch is a blocked double door. Although the opening has been blocked in the large room to the east, a pair of double red-painted doors remain. These are set at the level of the concrete floor slab. This may indicate that they pre-date the insertion of the suspended floor, or that they were accessed from a step in the suspended floor. If Warsaw Pact forces had moved to occupy West Berlin, the Teufelsberg would have been one of their most valuable prizes – a complex full of the latest western computer equipment. In addition to the small arms held to defend the site it was rumoured that explosive demolition charges were incorporated into its foundations to prevent it falling into Soviet hands (Behling and Jüttemann 2011, 32).

On the ground floor, to either end of the building, were two large, now L-shaped workrooms. To the east a ramp brought the lobby floor level up to that of the suspended floor and through an enclosed lobby into the eastern room. In the lobby a set of double doors in its south walls gave access to a room to the south that was probably originally separated from the larger room to the east. As noted above, this building has been heavily stripped and little may be reconstructed of its original form. Some of the few remains include traces of metal framing that held wooden panelling to some of the walls. To the west the large workroom was also entered through a similar lobby. Here there has been a later modification where the southern doorway has been bricked up and a small grilled window with a small narrow gap at its base inserted. This may have been used to oversee entry and for passing messages to a secure communications centre. The doors here are at floor level and open into the lobby, indicating in the western room there was either a ramp or set of steps to rise to the level of the now removed suspended floor. As with the other room, it has been thoroughly stripped, although odd traces of wall framing and wooden panelling survive. Also surviving on one wall is a dual voltage power socket for 110V American equipment and 220V German equipment (Figure 5.61). The floors on either side were covered in linoleum tiles and small circular cement and glue marks indicate the position of the feet of the suspended floor. This was based on a 62cm (2ft) square grid.

The upper two floors have also been comprehensively stripped, including their external walls. Both floors were also covered in linoleum tiles and as

Figure 5.61 1458. Ground floor. Dual German and American power sockets
Source: authors

on the ground floor small circular marks indicate the position of suspended floors (Figure 5.62 and 5.63). In front of the lift entrance on each floor the doors are level with the main floor surface, which implies there were steps or ramps leading up to the raised suspended floors. In some areas rectangular patterns of black and white tile scars were evident, in some areas corresponding to remaining black and duck-egg coloured tiles (Figure 5.64). It is unclear if they represent an earlier phase of use, perhaps predating the insertion of the suspended floors and marking the position of computer cabinets.

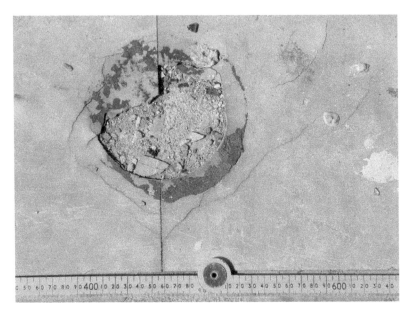

Figure 5.62 1458, scar left by a suspended floor support
Source: authors

Figure 5.63 1458, first floor, plug sockets
Source: authors

As discussed above, it was intended to convert this building into apartments and in the northeast corner of the second floor a wooden mock-up of an apartment was installed. Work was also started on dividing the upper floors into two bay units with pre-cast building blocks (Figure 5.65), although it has also been suggested that these were built as panels to encourage

Figure 5.64 1458. Patterns in the linoleum tiles may reveal the earlier layout of computer cabinets. Small circular marks indicate the position of legs for the later suspended floor

Source: authors

Figure 5.65 1458, first floor with later partitions possibly constructed during a scheme to convert the building into apartments

Source: authors

interventions by artists. Curiously, in some areas the walls appear to have been built directly on top of the linoleum floor.

From roof level the central concrete lift shaft and external staircase continues for a further five storeys and also supports circular cantilevered external platforms (Figure 5.66). Externally these were clad in a man-made fibre covering supported by an aluminium frame (Figure 5.67). At roof level the lift opens on to the base of the tower, part of which is covered by linoleum tiles (Figure 5.68).

Figure 5.66 1458, central lift tower, platform 4 with air-conditioning unit
Source: authors

Figure 5.67 1458, central lift tower, platform, fabric covering
Source: authors

Figure 5.68 1458, central lift tower, from the roof level
Source: Angus Boulton

To the east these are light green and to the north brown, indicating different functional areas on this level, some of which were partitioned by wire
grills. The lift doors also gave access to what was a T-shaped covered way
that linked the western and eastern radomes, both of which sit on low circular, concrete walls (Figures 5.69 and 5.70). Each of these housed a 12m
diameter parabolic antenna (Beckmann et al. 2011, 41). The low concrete
base walls for the geodesic domes are about 12m in diameter (Figure 5.71).

Internally, except for small electrical switch boxes, most of their fittings
have been stripped. In the centre of each dome was the mounting block
for the rotating antennae. To the east the antenna was mounted on a raised
central plinth 1.86m in diameter. The outer part was covered in asphalt
sheeting that also covers the floor of this dome. Inside is a slightly raised
concrete ring 0.65m in diameter and set into this are ten bolts with a 0.44m
diameter. At their centre is a small circular brass orientation plug with an
inscribed north-south line. The western dome has a grey painted floor and
at its centre a raised circular concrete plinth 1.9m in diameter with eight
mounting bolts.

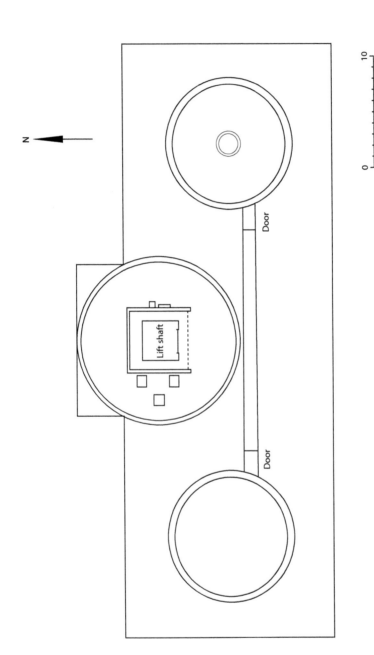

N

Door

Door

Lift shaft

Metres

0   10

Figure 5.69 1458, roof plan

Source: authors

Figure 5.70 1458, eastern radome
Source: authors

Figure 5.71 1458. Interior of the eastern radome showing the holdfast for the rotating surveillance equipment
Source: authors

Each of the tower's platforms could be accessed directly from the lift and the staircase. Each was also used to mount surveillance devices, and bolts on their surfaces mark the position of this equipment (Figure 5.72). On each of the levels, further orientation plugs are set into the surface of the platforms. Equipment was lifted onto the platforms through double doors on the tower's north side, which were present on all levels except for the upper one. The doors are missing, but metal ceiling runners indicate their positions. On the fourth level an electric crane survives. On the western side of this level is a large, hinged steel plate that allowed equipment to be transferred between the platforms. Also on the eastern side of the fourth platform is an air-conditioning unit. On the eastern side of the tower a metal cable conduit passes down from the radome through a rectangular hole in each platform to the main building. To its north on each platform is a smaller hole that has sub-sequently been blocked. On the upper level the stairs opened on to a raised rectangular platform 6.9m × 5.5m with a central 3.5m plate which seals the position of the equipment bay for the rotating radar or surveillance device. The surrounding surface is covered with asphalt. To the west is another small crane that allowed equipment to be raised from the floor beneath. On this top level was originally a rotating 10m parabolic antenna covered by a radome and above it a smaller dome housing a 4m antenna (Figure 5.73 and 5.74).

Figure 5.72 1458. Central lift tower, platform 2. Bolts on platforms indicate the position of surveillance devices and a line on the brass stud marks the north-to-south alignment

Source: authors

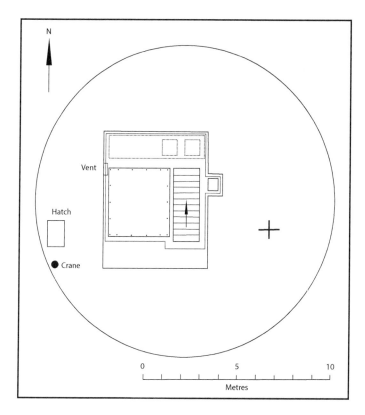

Figure 5.73 1458, plan of upper radome interior

Source: authors

Figure 5.74 1458, upper radome interior

Source: authors

There was a plan for the Deutsche Flugsicherung (DFS) (air traffic control) to reuse the tower to control Berlin's airspace. The original radome on the main tower was removed and replaced for this purpose in 1999, but the scheme was later abandoned (Beckmann et al. 2011, 116).

1453 Dining Facility

As described above, on entering the site the first major building to be encountered is the Dining Facility or mess [1453] (Figure 5.75). Except for some of the smaller kitchen facilities in the operations buildings, this was the principal dining facility and was jointly used by British and American military personnel of all ranks, and civilian employees. The facility was run by the US Army and ran for 24 hours a day providing meals for the thousand-plus personnel who worked on the site (Bowman 1997). American personnel who worked the 'mids' shift, 12pm to 8am, complained about a monotonous daily diet of grilled ham-and-cheese sandwiches (Wood nd, 11), while the British were bemused by the white gravy, cold tea and grits (Manton 2015, 148–149).

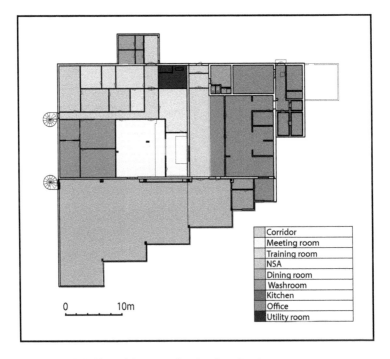

	Corridor
	Meeting room
	Training room
	NSA
	Dining room
	Washroom
	Kitchen
	Office
	Utility room

0 _____ 10m

Figure 5.75 1453. Plan of the mess showing functional areas

Source: Redrawn from plan provided by Berlin Technical University on Field Station Berlin by Katharina Beckmann, David Derksen, Robert Haesecke-Diesing and Florian Leitner

The Dining Facility is a two-phase building initially constructed between 1969 and 1971 and later extended between 1978 and 1982. An air photograph taken in July 1971 shows that the original building was complete by this date (Figure 3.7). This was a rectangular, two-storey structure dug into a terrace on the southern side of the hill. The basement area is of reinforced concrete and the upper storey is carried on a heavy steel frame. The exterior walls of the upper storey are infilled with bree- zeblocks and clad in sheeting and were windowless. The basement is an open store area ten bays in width with a platform loading bay on its south side (Figure 5.76).

In 1971 there were two wide loading bays and two single personnel doors to the east. At some point the eastern loading bay has been bricked up, although its position remains visible as a wall scar. Today, on enter- ing through the main entrance, immediately to the left is a self-contained plant room. Beyond this on the west wall are wooden stairs that led to a now removed wooden walkway, its position indicated by wooden batons fixed to the west and north walls. A number of wall-mounted heaters also

Figure 5.76 1453. The lower loading area 53.0.01 with the loading platform to the right

Source: authors

survive. Yellow painted lines of the store floor mark the position of storage areas and clear access ways. In the southeast corner scars on the walls and floor mark the position of an enclosed office. A single door in its east wall leads to a washroom and the door in its south wall onto the loading platform. The easternmost two bays are separated from the main storage area by a wall and the enclosed area is accessed through a pair of sliding pale blue doors. Each of these is adorned with a picture of the cartoon cat Garfield, extolling the health and safety messages of 'Don't pussyfoot around [-] wear your steel toes' and 'Keep your vision [-] wear your goggles'. Within this area are steel racks and cages, which were presumably used to secure more valuable items. To the south of the loading bays the extension of the Dining Facility created a triangular-shaped, covered loading area and parking place. This is open, although secured by wire screens. Entry into this area was through a roller shutter door. The stores were essential to ensure the continuous operation of the facility and 11,000 items were kept on its inventory (Bowman 1997).

The late 1970s extension abuts the southern wall of the original building. The southern face of the extension is stepped and over sails the front of the stores' loading area (Figure 5.77). The western and eastern walls are solid, while to the south are large windows that offer panoramic views over Berlin's western suburbs. After the Dining Facility was extended it was essentially divided into three self-contained areas. To the east were the kitchens, to the south a large open dining area and to the northwest, occupying about two-thirds of the original building, were a briefing room, offices and training rooms. The Dining Facility is entered through an unprepossessing single door in its north wall. Internally are two sets of double doors and to the east a washroom with toilets and a shower. Once through the second set of doors there is a large lobby that was originally divided by handrails, the positions of whose feet are visible on the floor. To the east is a large self-service counter and behind that on the east wall scars mark the positions of the cooking ranges. Above these on the roof are a number of vents and extractor fans. Vents shown in this position on the July 1971 air photograph probably indicate the kitchen is in its original position. To the rear of the servery three openings give access to food preparation and storage areas. In the northeast corner of the original building is a plant room and to the east an extension has been added with storerooms. The current plant room door and the doorway to the extension are both shown as original exterior doors on the 1971 photograph. This also shows a vent over the plant room, confirming that this is also an original feature. All the kitchen and associated corridors are finished in rectangular brown and yellow tiles, while the storeroom interiors have white tiles. In the extension immediately to the south of the kitchen are two rooms that probably acted as administrative offices, although a serving hatch in the wall of the western room may indicate

Figure 5.77 1453. The south front of the mess from the east
Source: authors

a bar or drinks servery. At the south end of the lobby, double doors gave access
to the main Dining Facility (Figure 5.78).

This is a single open space, although there was a partition at its eastern end.
It is unclear if this would have formed a dining area, or perhaps a seating area,
as it also provided access to the entrance lobby and the rooms to the east. At

Figure 5.78 1453. Mess, main dining area
Source: authors

the eastern side two squares of red carpet and a central area with ceiling ventilation hood may mark the position of a self-service food stand. In the west
wall a single door gives access to an emergency spiral staircase. To the west,
scars on the floor indicate the positions of partitions in the dining area. It was
also noted that earlier brown plastic flooring had later been covered by carpet.

During the extension, the northwest section of the building was probably extensively reconfigured internally. A new entrance porch was added
to the west of the main canteen entrance. This comprises a lobby and two
toilets, to the west. From the lobby, double doors give access to an L-shaped
corridor, and at its western end a door leads to an emergency spiral staircase. Immediately on entering through the double doors on the east side is a
coat and hat rail. The corridor separates the rooms into two blocks: a group
of seven small offices to the northwest and an L-shaped group of rooms
to the east and south. The group to the northwest were used for training
and National Security Agency offices (Beckmann et al. 2011, 096). Two
detached doors in this area display Garfield cartoons: one shows Garfield
wearing a crown with the text 'Property book office', and the other shows
him wearing a safety hat with the motto 'A mind is too important to waste,
wear your helmet' (Figure 5.79). To their south, the field station's manager

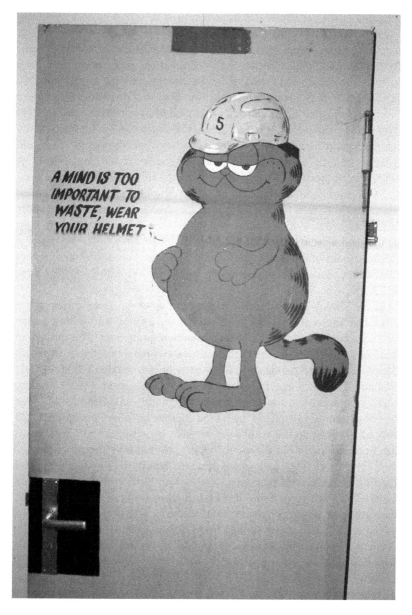

Figure 5.79 1453. Mess, a Garfield cartoon – 'A mind is too important to waste, wear your helmet' – on a door in Room 53.0.29

Source: authors

and administrative team occupied four offices. In these offices seniority is reflected by the use of wooden wainscoting.

In its latest phase, the Dining Facility was also used for briefings and meetings. From the main gate [1462] important visitors to the Dining Facility building might be directed to the adjacent car park without any need to enter the more secure parts of the facility. Despite the facility's highly sensitive activities, liaison with other American and British agencies based in Europe and their home countries was vital to its operations, and in 1988 over 1000 visits were hosted at the site (Bowman 1997). Regular visitors included people concerned with the day-to-day operation of the base, and other western personnel attending training courses or briefing sessions. A reflection of the station's importance was the number of high-level visitors who were briefed on the facility's capabilities. These included United States Congressmen from various intelligence committees, senior military personnel and in 1988, 30 top-level intelligence personnel who held their annual conference at the Teufelsberg (Bowman 1997). The Operational Record Books of the British 26 Signals Unit also record many senior visitors, although some names remain redacted (TNA: AIR 29/4578 8 June 1977, 1).

In the Dining Facility to the east of the block of seven offices are a large briefing room with a raised dais along its east wall with a screen behind, and a room to its rear for projection equipment. The projection has black painted walls and at the rear of the room a raised dais on which the projection and perhaps sound equipment was mounted. Images were probably projected against a now removed glass screen. On the briefing room side a curtain, the rail for which remains, could shield this. The briefing room has secondary panelling comprising blue floor carpet taken part of the way up the wall, with wooden panelling above. Where this has been stripped from the west wall the original blue and white painted wall finish is visible. On a pair of detached boards in this room is another Garfield cartoon with the legend 'Just try to do it without us'. A board on the east wall records the last units stationed at the Teufelsberg. The briefing room could be entered from the main access corridor and doors to the south gave access to the Dining Facility. North of the projection room was another training room and to its north a small frame room for telecommunications equipment and a larger room whose function is unknown.

After the closure of the Teufelsberg, the building has been partly stripped and from the evidence of abandoned mattresses and clothing and graffiti, it is regularly used as a squat and party venue (Figure 5.80). This is discussed further in Chapter 7, 'Closure'.

Figure 5.80 1453. Mess, eastern end of main dining area decorated by squatters
Source: authors

Summary

Uniquely, so far as the authors are aware, this chapter has presented a detailed functional description of a Cold War intelligence-gathering centre, operational at the height of the Cold War. By characterising the buildings and reading significance and functionality into all spaces that comprise the Teufelsberg, a clear picture has emerged of process, information flow, operational connections and divisions and the distinction between social and operational space, US and British space and space occupied by offices, industrial scale computing and for social and professional interaction. The study also revealed some icons of Cold War myth and reality: two-way mirrors, Faraday cages and the shredding and pulping of primary data. The next chapter will summarise these findings in terms of architecture and the site's technical provision, before drawing some wider comments and conclusions about the study, and observations of the site's afterlife.

6 Architectural summary and overview

Architecture

Signals intelligence is one of the most secretive areas of government, and prior to this study very little information on post-war intelligence gathering has entered into the public domain. The ruined buildings of the Teufelsberg offered a rare if not unique opportunity to study the architecture of a relatively modern intelligence-gathering centre, one developed to house vast banks of data processing machines. As this study has shown, an archaeological analysis of complex modern technological sites can stimulate considerations of the social history of the facility, how movement was controlled and activities within buildings were divided into distinctive zones. It can also reveal something of the technologies that were used and how they were housed. What it cannot reveal are the secrets of the software, nor what was intercepted.

The Teufelsberg was one of the West's most important listening stations. Its location and presence was impossible to hide. Instead the operational buildings hid in plain sight behind plain facades finished in a neutral blue and white colour scheme. For almost the first decade of its operation, equipment was housed in mobile facilities that were gradually replaced by pre-fabricated buildings. One of the earliest specialised buildings to be erected was a pneumatic dome covering a radar or other type of surveillance device. These became known as 'arctic domes' after their deployment in the late 1950s to protect the radars of the North American arctic Distant Early Warning (DEW) line. This term was also applied to protective geodesic domes that were designed by the American architect-engineer Buckminster Fuller, and were 75 percent non-metallic and covered in fibreglass panels that are pervious to radar and radio emissions, while offering weather protection and concealment (Maniaque 2008, 94–99). Around the globe, these distinctive domed sentinels marked the edge of the western world.

By the late 1960s, such was the intelligence-gathering value of the Teufelsberg that America and the United Kingdom embarked on a massive

construction programme to vastly increase its ability to collect and analyse data. The Americans added the main operations building, a large three-
storey building, capped by three radomes, one set on a five-storey tower.
To its south the British built a large two-storey building. Both were windowless and designed primarily for accommodating electronic surveillance
equipment and perhaps large mainframe computers for analysing the gathered data. This sensitive equipment both required a carefully controlled
environment and, in the case of the Teufelsberg, shielding from counter-
surveillance. Each of these buildings was built on a heavy steel frame to
support concrete floors. Initially, evidence from photographs of the interior
of the British Building M and patterns and marks of the linoleum floor tiles
in the main American building [1458] suggests first-generation equipment
was placed directly on the floors of these buildings. In the late 1970s and
early 1980s, coinciding with the construction of the new analysts building
[1475], the whole facility appears to have been refurbished and upgraded.
The original buildings appear to have been refitted and it was probably at
this time that they were fitted with supported suspended floors. This probably reflected a major technological upgrade for the facility as new digital
computer technology replaced the earlier systems dominated by electro-
mechanical equipment. Beneath the floors snaked thousands of wires to
link the machines and air-conditioning conduits to remove the excess heat,
which was also removed with further conditioning conduits within the deep
suspended ceilings.

From the evidence of building [1437A], one of the few surviving 1960s
buildings, internal decor in the 1960s and 1970s included painted horizontal-
striped light and dark blue walls and a stairwell finished in garish brown,
yellow and orange bands. Probably during the late 1970s refurbishment and
early 1980s construction campaigns, the internal finish of this building was
considerably enhanced with timber sheet wainscoting and wood panelling
that is characteristic of the high decorative standards of many 1980s United
States military installations seen elsewhere by the authors. Another feature
is the use of brown gloss paint on metalwork and doors. Many areas were
also covered by carpeted suspended floor tiles, although in other areas linoleum and cork floor finishes may relate to local technical requirements.
In contrast, most contemporary British military facilities have a more aus-
tere appearance with painted walls and plain linoleum or tiled floors. They
stand in even greater difference with their Warsaw Pact equivalents, where
crude gloss-paint wall finishes were typical, decorated linoleum commonplace and heavily patterned wallpaper often a sign of distinction. During
the 1980s, murals became more prevalent on United States bases, but are
rare on the Teufelsberg, with one wall-sized example in the military police
area and occasional defaced unit 'zaps' surviving elsewhere. In the Dining

Facility building the cartoon character Garfield was used to convey health and safety messages, and was probably associated with the station's maintenance crews.

Technical equipment

The manufacturer's nameplates on the few surviving pieces of technical equipment often confirm the date of installation and the location of the supplier. In common with practice elsewhere, less specialised plant, such as air-conditioning equipment, was sourced from the host country, a policy that reduced the initial procurement and ongoing maintenance costs. Most of the interior fittings in the computer areas, including the suspended access floors and ceilings, were also sourced from German suppliers. For example, on the second floor lobby of building [1475] is a Siemens Brandschutzsystem SRS 150 cabinet. In a number of areas dual electricity sockets are found that supplied electricity at the local German 220 voltage and the lower American 110 voltage. In the British area, no United Kingdom type plugs were noted, probably indicating that any of its British supplied equipment was able to tolerate the local supply.

The specialist monitoring apparatus used by the British was a mixture of military and civilian equipment. Across the four decades from 1950, communications technology evolved from glass valve and transistor electronic circuits, supported by electro-mechanical systems, to the forerunners of modern digital systems. During this period, as communications systems became smaller, lighter and more robust, increasing amounts of communications equipment became commonplace amongst all Warsaw Pact formations, vastly increasing the potential to gather electronic intelligence. It was an increase matched in computer processing power to analyse the huge amounts of collected data. No definitive list survives for all the monitoring equipment used by the western allies in Berlin; some is mentioned on websites and in official returns see pages 57–58, although for the 1970s and 1980s some of this information is still withheld. At Gatow in about 1960 the Royal Signals Unit was using an Eddystone 770R receiver. This 19 valve set was manufactured in Birmingham and with a large linear display and flywheel assisted tuning was particularly suited to radio monitoring. Later in the 1960s, standard military Larkspur series transistor based R216 receivers were in use. Many other pieces of equipment were professional civilian types including the Ferrograph tape recorders, Ampex VR 650 video-recorders, RE301 recorders and Hewlett-Packard 3950 tape recorders. British and American companies supplied most of these items, but West German firms also supplied some equipment. This included the 120m tall antenna on the Teufelsberg, supplied by Munich-based Rohde and Schwarz, who also produced another antenna for use at Gatow. Siemens T100 teleprinters were also widely used. As discussed above, there is less information on the equipment used in the later decades. By the 1980s an American supplied Digital Equipment Corporation VAX computer system was in use at Gatow, and was a system used elsewhere in West Germany by the United States military. For internal security, home-supplied pick-resistant locks by Sargents and Greenleaf, United States, and Ingersoll, United Kingdom, were often preferred.

Summary

This chapter has highlighted the significance of an archaeological approach, through its ability to track process and production through, for example, the nameplates on plant that has survived site clearance. The study has also started to reveal the working conditions and the decor, and how this varied between the American and British operational areas. As further such studies of the period are undertaken across the wider NATO landscape (see Cocroft and Thomas 2003 for an example), the contextual background to each study becomes clearer, and comparisons and contradictions between sites will become more obvious.

7   Closure

Afterlife

With the opening of the Berlin Wall in November 1989, German reunification in the following year and the subsequent break-up of the Soviet Union, the role of the Field Station came to an end. On Thursday 16 January 1992, the United States' operational units of Field Station Berlin were stood down and the facility given over to the Closure Task Force (Dowdee 1992, 1). The RAF's 26 Signals Unit remained operational here for slightly longer, until midnight on Saturday 29 February 1992. The following six months were spent dismantling equipment and on 11 August its facilities were handed over to the United States Army (Taylor 2003, 223). The formal withdrawal of the wartime allies from the city took place in 1994, although elements of 26 Signals Unit remained at Gatow until March 1995 (Taylor 2003, 223). In 1999, the Teufelsberg hosted a conference, 'On the Front Lines of the Cold War', a meeting of former CIA and KGB officers and other intelligence experts, although the British were noticeably absent. It formed a fitting venue for these former opponents to exchange reminiscences about some of most high-profile cases from the opening decades of the Cold War (Wallace 1999; Steury 2000, 1–10).

The point has now been reached where the Teufelsberg has spent more time as derelict structures than as operational units, and all now have complex post-abandonment biographies. On withdrawal the buildings were thoroughly stripped of all equipment and fittings that might afford hostile intelligence services with clues about the facility's operational capabilities. In the late 1990s, the developers Gruhl and Partner proposed converting the former listening station into a hotel and luxury apartments marketed under the banner 'Resort Teufelsberg Berlin'. This scheme came to nothing, but it did result in some demolition, especially at the eastern end of the site, and stripping of the building interiors was started. Also on the second floor of the main building [1458], a timber mock-up of one of the proposed apartments was created. To the east the concrete foundations of a large circular basement car park were started and to its north is a large rectangular foundation slab.

Like most archaeological sites, the Teufelsberg has a clear stratigraphy, reminiscent of Near Eastern tells, where deposits accumulate into hills over the course of millennia. Here the 'tell' is entirely contemporary comprising, in one site, much of the story of twentieth-century Berlin. Across the ground surface in many parts of the Teufelsberg lie shattered fragments of building stones and bricks and small pieces of pottery and tiles. Most of this wartime rubble was cleared by hand in a time of acute material shortage, where any reuseable building materials and objects were taken up and recycled. What ended up on the Teufelsberg was the unusable rubble, rubble which now overlies the unfinished and bomb-damaged remains of Speer's university, which provided a firm foundation for the mound that become known as Teufelsberg. Intelligence gathered here during the site's Cold War phase of occupation was pulped, incinerated and removed while, as we have seen, given its secretive operations, on closure the facility was thoroughly stripped of all objects that might reveal its functions. The site now forms a backdrop to techno parties and music videos, a research and creative space for academics, planners and artists and a (not so) blank canvas for street artists. For all of these diverse communities, along with those more formalised groups who came before them, this is a highly significant place, valued for its history, as an iconic landmark, for its alternative character and for the opportunities to explore. Discard and abandonment are recurring themes, but these processes have only added to its appeal. The site has very quickly become a shell, devoid of many of the traces of its former occupants. It remains, however, a site in use, and with a future, whatever that might be.

This is not therefore a site only experiencing 'net loss'. Increasingly numerous and visible are the objects brought *to* the site by the many transient groups and individuals who have spent time here subsequent to its post Cold War abandonment, and the artworks created here. Abandoned mattresses, clothing, a child's buggy and a sitting area with a campfire reveal the presence of squatters in the former Dining Facility [1453], while the Jambalaya radome building [1465] has been used as a longer-term squat. Discarded records and record and compact disc sleeves bear witness to past raves and techno parties, part of a scene that had social significance particularly as the wall came down and young people from formerly East and West Berlin began the task of forming a unified city once again (Schofield and Rellensmann 2015). Unused G8 protest posters from 2011 indicate some connection with protestors. What survives on the surface of the site, therefore, bears an oddly unconventional relationship to the military activities conducted here between the 1960s and 1990s.

Casual vandalism has also taken its toll and virtually all windows on the site are smashed, the material covering of the radome tower is ripped, interior walls demolished and fires have destroyed some areas. A more systematic approach has also been taken to removing more valuable metals. The formerly copper-lined rooms have been stripped and the floors ripped up to gain access to the wiring conduits, leaving only their stripped plastic husks.

Virtually all the facility's accessible surfaces, as well as some in more challenging locations, are covered in graffiti. Around 2010, artists associated with the Tascheles Collective established Projekt Teufelsberg, centred on the Dining Facility [1453] (Figure 7.1) and the Jambalaya Tower [1465] (Figure 5.28). Traces of their venture include abandoned canvasses in the Dining Facility, the decoration of a serving hatch with dismantled audio equipment, and the stencilling of 'Camp Delta 4' on a wall in the serving area. Outside of the Dining Facility, scrap metal has been turned into an impromptu sculpture park, and 'Projekt Teufelsberg' signs placed on the Dining Facility wall and Jambalaya tower. This technological ruin dominating Berlin's skyline has thus passed deep into the city's counter and artistic cultures. The site provides the backdrop for Scooter's (2009) *Under the*

Figure 7.1 1453. Mess, north wall of Projekt Teufelsberg, established by the Tacheles Collective around 2010

Source: authors

Figure 7.2 1465. Close to the Jamabalaya tower, traces of a techno party, a scatter of records and other objects

Source: authors

Radar Over the Top album, while other musical connections include Youan-dewan's (2010) *Meet Me at Teufelsberg*. Websites describe the site's special character as a techno party venue, a role that has created its own archaeological record (Figure 7.2).

The ruins are also a striking film location and have appeared in *The Gambler* (2007), David Sieveking's 2010 exploration of the Transcendental Meditation Movement *David Wants to Fly* and in the vampire movie *We Are the Night* (2010). The material traces of the site's use as a movie set were described in Chapter 5. The site has been brilliantly recreated by impressive CGI, for the German TV mini-series *Der gleiche Himmel* (2017), later shown on Netflix as *The Same Sky*.

The facility has gained international repute amongst the urban explorer community and attracts many unauthorised visitors who post their experiences online. They have also marked their visits by ubiquitous beer cans, bottles and cigarette packets and other discarded objects that testify to its international fame. More recently the security firm eMGe has undertaken to secure the site in return for film and photography rights. In May 2012, Shalmon Abraham (artist and leader of Verein Berliner Teufelsberg, Association of Berlin Teufeslberg) took over the lease with a view to encouraging artistic use of the site. To cater for the growing fascination with the place, organised tours are available. New plans for the site are frequently proposed and vigorously debated.

Significance

Today the Teufelsberg represents a rare technological ruin of facilities that during the 1970s and 1980s housed one of the most powerful computer complexes in the world. They were built at a time when this powerful computing technology was essentially the domain of government and the development of the technology was being stimulated by the demands of the Cold War and the state spending necessary to counter its threats. In this context, the Teufelsberg may also lay claim to be home of the modern information age, when in 1981 one of its computers is reputed to have sent the first transatlantic email (Durie 2012, 102).

Throughout the Cold War, the Teufelsberg and associated intelligence-gathering sites in West Berlin continuously harvested electronic emissions from the Soviet and East German forces that surrounded them. It was ideally placed to intercept military and governmental radio traffic, telephone conversations, microwave communications and later satellite transmissions. As we have seen, the types of data gathered here divide into two main categories. First, military theatre or tactical information, including the order of battle of opposing forces, their readiness states, frequencies of radio and radar networks and types and capabilities of equipment deployed. Second, high-level party and political communications that at times of tension could provide a crucial advantage during negotiations, as well as realistic assessments of the state of the East German economy. In these terms, the site was vital in gauging the Warsaw Pact's intentions and ensuring a proportionate response by the West. Precise information on the Teufelsberg's targets and the effect it had on British and western policy has yet to be released, and information is also unavailable on the level of co-operation between the British and American units, and if they specialised in targeting different sources of data. When and if further details of its intercepts are released, they may revolutionise our understanding of the Cold War, as much as the revelations in the 1970s about the cracking of the German Enigma codes at Bletchley Park, Buckinghamshire, England, did for our comprehension of the Second World War. But for now the site is all we have, including the physical remnants of the buildings constructed and the facilities installed within them. For now, therefore, the archaeological approach described here provides the best opportunity for making sense of the Teufelsberg, and shedding new light on this crucial and little-understood phase of Berlin's fascinating and troubled history. The fieldwork described here provides this unique record.

The project also has significance as the first detailed archaeological investigation of a recent digital-era signals intelligence site. Although the methods used have been developed elsewhere, they were refined for this study. As an example, and taking the earlier statement about the relationships between US and British operations 'on the ground' as its hypothesis, analysis of access routes revealed that there was minimal physical contact between the operations of the Americans and the British, in spite of the 'special relationship' that existed then (as now) between these allies. Furthermore, mapping false floors, the types of flooring and lowered ceilings (as evidence of air conditioning required for computer hardware) revealed functional spaces within the Teufelsberg. These detailed observations provide an unique understanding of the way these vitally significant buildings were used, and by whom.

The archaeological examination of the Teufelsberg is therefore both unique and timely. The methodology provides a bespoke and distinctly archaeological approach to the investigation of secretive signals intelligence sites from the recent past. This approach may be the only method to studying such installations where information is hard to obtain and very rarely in the public domain. It would also seem an appropriate method for other high-tech information processing centres comparable to the Teufelsberg where access provides the opportunity for such close scrutiny.

The future

The future of the Teufelsberg is hard to predict. Most would probably agree that complete demolition would be unwelcome, given the values attached to the site by all interest groups. The challenge is that these values are both diverse and often exist in direct contradiction with one another. How does one create a compromise between those favouring a formal museum or study centre (a 'campus' almost), a reuse perhaps as a hotel or leisure facility, and those favouring a more creative and fluid space? There are also those who like it just the way it is, as a place for urban exploration, trespass, youthful excitement and adventure. Should we ignore the site's difficult heritage: its Nazi origins, or the fact of an allied site being constructed on top of a pile of war rubble? And how can informed decisions about the site's future be made, where the interest groups are so diverse, comprising former servicemen and linguists from the US and the UK ('the veterans if you will'), city planners and members of alternative and hard-to-reach communities? Should one set of viewpoints be given priority over another, and if so how is that decision made? The site has now been in alternative use longer than it was a secret military establishment, and the alternative community is at least local; for the British and Americans who worked here, this is an 'orphan heritage', a small part of British or US heritage on foreign soil.

As this book is finally prepared for publication, the news has been announced of its protection as a monument, placing it under 'Denkmalschutz', or monument protection by the Landesdenkmalamts or State Monuments Office (eg www.berliner-zeitung.de/berlin/teufelsberg-ex-abhoeranlage-steht-nun-unter-denkmalschutz-31540932, retrieved 9 November 2018). No one doubts the justification for this. As Culture Senator Klaus Lederer describes it: 'Der Teufelsberg ist ein einzigartiges und vielschichtiges Geschichtsdenkmal des 20. Jahrhunderts, das in dieser Art wohl nur in Berlin – als Hauptstadt des Nazireichs und geteilter Stadt im Kalten Krieg – entstehen konnte' (trans: 'The Teufelsberg is a unique and multi-layered historical monument of the twentieth century, which could only exist in Berlin – as the capital of the Nazi Empire and divided city in the Cold War'). But inevitably the decision is contested. On the one hand, protection may prevent further deterioration; but on the other, it constrains options for its future use, and arguably favours a move towards formalising and placing restriction on what has become renowned as a creative and anarchic space, highly characteristic of the city in which it is located. Indeed it follows in the spirit of Lederer's observation (above) that Teufelsberg as a Cold War installation could only have existed in Berlin. This is also true (and arguably more so) of the post Cold War Teufelsberg.

This study has sought to both promote and demonstrate all aspects of the site's significance, and to different communities of interest. For a more conventional archaeological site with multiple layers of occupation evidence, one would not generally identify one single layer as having more value than others. Usually the significance of archaeological sites (tells, let's say) is in the entire history, the sequence of occupation phases and how the site developed over time. Just as an archaeological approach was taken to develop our understanding of the Teufelsberg, an archaeological approach to significance may also be relevant, providing an inclusive and robust framework for deciding a sustainable future in which multiple uses and users can be present, whether guided by or in spite of its protection.

Bibliography

Primary sources

The National Archives, Kew

AIR 2/17557 Unit badge of No.5 signals wing 29 March 1965–7 July 1970.

AIR 28/1207 RAF Gatow (Berlin) January 1956–December 1960.

AIR 28/1584 Gatow BFPO 45 January 1961–December 1965.

AIR 28/2014 Gatow 1 January 1966–31 December 1968.

AIR 28/2016 Gatow 1 January 1971–31 December 1975.

AIR 28/2215 Gatow 1 January 1976–31 December 1980.

AIR 29/3881 No.26 Signals Unit, RAF Gatow September 1966–December 1970.

AIR 29/4332 No.26 Signals Unit, RAF Gatow January 1971–December 1975.

AIR 29/4578 No.26 Signals Berlin 1 January 1976–31 December 1980.

AIR 29/4927 No.26 Signals Unit, RAF Gatow, Germany 1981–1982.

AIR 34/576 Berlin: Spandau BMW engine works: Target information January 1943–November 1944.

DEFE 44/473 An assessment of the Type 37F engine based on the Berlin Firebar exploitation August 1967.

FO 1060/4690 Building on the Teufelsberg West Berlin: Additional requirements for purposes of the United States Army 1 January 1964–31 December 1964.

FO 1060/5191 Teufelsberg West Berlin: Requisitioned area budget 1 January 1968–31 December 1968.

FO 1060/5536 Radio Mast at Teufelsberg West Berlin 1 January 1976–31 December 1976.

WO 32/20353 Cpl B. Patchett Defection to East Berlin 1963–1964.

WO 305/854 13 Signal Regiment April 1959–March 1960.

WO 305/2011 13 Signal Regiment April 1960–March 1965.

WO 305/2417 13 Signal Regiment workshop April 1964–March 1965.

WO 305/3432 13 Signal Regiment 1968–1970.

Royal Commission on the Ancient and Historical Monuments of Scotland – TARA air photography

TW2972 J/357 541 Sqdn, frame 3240, 20 February 1944.

Bundesbeauftragte für die Stasi-Unterlagen (BstU)
Archive der Zentralstelle

MfS-HA II 26 Signals Unit Number 34747 pages 0022–0031 9 August 1978.

MfS-HA II 26 Signals Unit Number 34747 Document 32072/25/84 pages 0256–0258.

Secondary sources

Aldrich, R. J. 2001 'CGHQ and Sigint in the early Cold War, 1945–70' *Intelligence and National Security* 16 (1) 67–96.

Aldrich, R. J. 2010 *GCHQ: The uncensored story of Britain's most secret intelligence agency* London: Harper Press.

Altner, H. 2005 *Berlin dance of death* Staplehurst: Spellmount.

Anderson, B. 2017 *Buried city, unearthing Teufelsberg: Berlin and its geography of forgetting* London and New York: Routledge.

Beckmann, K., Derksen, D., Haesecke-Diesing, R. and Leitner, F. 2011 *Field station Berlin* MA thesis, Berlin Technical University.

Beckmann, K., Derksen, D., Haesecke-Diesing, R. and Leitner, F. 2013 *Field station Berlin Geheime Abhörstation auf dem Teufelsberg* Berlin: Berliner Unterwelten.

Beevor, A. 2002 *Berlin downfall 1945* London: Penguin.

Behling, K. and Jüttemann, A. 2011 *Der Berliner Teufelsberg: Trümmer, Truppen und Touristen* Berlin: Berlin Story.

Bowman, S. L. 1997 *Teufelsberg, Berlin and the Cold War* typescript report Allied Museum Berlin.

Carney, J. M. 2013 *Against all enemies: An American's Cold War journey* Amazon print on demand.

Cocroft, W. D. and Schofield, J. 2016 *Der Teufelsberg in Berlin Eine archäologische Bestandsaufnahme des westlichen Horchpostens im Kalten Krieg* Berlin: Ch.Links.

Cocroft, W. D. and Thomas, R. J. C. 2003 *Cold War building for nuclear confrontation 1946–1989* Swindon: English Heritage.

Cooper, D. M. 2002 *C Trick: Sort of a memoir* San Diego: Pale Bone Publishing.

Crowley, D. and Pavitt, J. 2008 *Cold War modern design 1945–1970* London: V & A Publishing.

Dowdee, S. 1992 'One team, one mission' *The Sentinel Command Information Field Station Berlin* 5 (2) 1.

Durie, W. 2012 *The British Garrison Berlin 1945–1994* Berlin: Verganenheitsverlag.

Eichner, K. and Dobbert, A. 1997 *Headquarters Germany Die USA-Geheimdienste in Deutschland* Berlin: edition ost.

Elliot, G. and Shukman, H. 2002 *Secret classrooms: An untold story of the Cold War* London: St Ermin's Press.

English Heritage 2008 *Conservation principles: Policies and guidance for the sustainable management of the historic environment* Swindon: English Heritage.

Faligot, R. 2001 'France, Sigint and the Cold War' *Intelligence and National Security* 16 (1) 177–208.

Geraghty, T. 1997 *Brixmis: The untold exploits of Britain's most daring Cold War spy mission* London: Harpers Collins.

Harrison, R. and Schofield, J. 2010 *After modernity: Archaeology of the contemporary past* Oxford: Oxford University Press.

Herrington, S. A. 1999 *Traitors among us: Inside the spy catcher's world* New York: Harcourt.

Historic England 2016 *Understanding historic buildings a guide to good recording practice* Swindon: Historic England.

Holbrook, J. R. 2008 *Potsdam mission memoir of a US Army intelligence officer in communist East Germany* Bloomington: Author House.

Isaacs, J. and Downing, T. 1998 *Cold War* London: Bantam Press.

Jackson, P. 2001 *Hambuhren Lower Saxony: A military history 1939–1999* Oxford: Privately Published.

Jackson, P. and Haysom, D. 2014 *Covert radar and signals interception: The career of Eric Ackermann* Barnsley: Pen & Sword.

Kellerhoff, S. F. and von Kostka, B. 2012 *Hauptstadt der Spione Geheimdienste in Berlin im Kalten Krieg* Berlin: Berlin Story.

Ladd, B. 1997 *The ghosts of Berlin confronting German history in the urban landscape* Chicago: Chicago Press.

Lake, M., Monckton, L. and Morrison, K. A. 2006 'Interpreting Bletchley Park' 49–57 in Schofield et al. 2006.

Mackris, K. 2008 *Seduced by secrets: Inside the Stasi's Spy-Tech World* New York: Cambridge University Press.

Maddrell, P. 2012 'British intelligence through the eyes of the Stasi: What the Stasi's records show about the operations of British intelligence in Cold War Germany' *Intelligence and National Security* 27 (1), 46–74.

Maniaque, C. 2008 'Cold War front lines: The architecture of defence' in Crowley and Pavitt, 94–99.

Manton, D. 2015 *I was a Cold War Penguin* Privately published Amazon.

Marsden, R. 1998 'Operation "Schooner/Nylon": RAF flying in the Berlin Control Zone' *Intelligence and National Security* 13 (4) 178–193.

Prock, J. 1992 'Soldier to soldier' *The Sentinel* 3 February.

Read, A. and Fisher, D. 1993 *The fall of Berlin* London: Pimilco.

Schmidt-Eenboom, E. 2001 'The Bundesnachrichtendienst, the Bundeswehr and Sigint in the Cold War and after' *Intelligence and National Security* 16 (1) 129–176.

Schofield, J. and Cocroft, W. (eds) 2007 *A fearsome heritage: Diverse legacies of the Cold War* Walnut Creek: Left Coast Press (One World Archaeology).

Schofield, J., Klausmeier, A. and Purbrick, L. (eds) 2006 *Re-mapping the field: New approaches in conflict archaeology* Berlin: Westkreuz-Verlag.

Schofield, J. and Rellensmann, L. 2015 'Underground heritage: Berlin techno and the changing city' *Heritage & Society* 8 (2) 111–138.

Schofield, J. and Schofield, A. E. Gp. Cpt. 2005 'Views of the wall: Allied perspectives' in Schmidt, L. and von Preuschen, H. (eds), *On both sides of the wall: Preserving monuments and sites of the Cold War era* 36–43 Berlin: Westkreuz-Verlag.

Smith, M. 2003 'Britain's secret jet crash Cold War coup' *The Telegraph* 26 December.

Stafford, D. 2002 *Spies beneath Berlin* London: John Murray.

Stenak, M., Pedersen, T. T., Hansen, P. H. and Jespersen, M. 2013 *Kold Krig* Kulturstyrelsen: Copenhagen.

Steury, D. P. 2000 'On the front lines of the Cold War: The intelligence war in Berlin' *Studies in Intelligence* 9 1–10.

Taylor, B. 2003 *Royal Air Force Germany since 1945* Hinckley: Midland.

Wallace, C. P. 1999 'How we spied on you' *Time* 154 (13) 27 September.

War Office 1949 *The Soviet Army Tactics and organisation* The War Office.

Williams, K. 2014 *The Teufelsberg Historic Site: A Preliminary Interpretation Plan* A thesis submitted in partial fulfilment of the requirements for the degree of Master of Arts, Brandenburg University of Technology, Cottbus.

Wolf, M. 1998 *Memoirs of a spymaster: The man who waged a secret war against the West* London: Pimlico.

Wood, J. nd 'Thoughts on the mids meal' newsletter at the Allied Museum Berlin.

Woodhead, L. 2005 *My life as a spy* London: MacMillan.

Wright, K. and Jefferies, P. 2015 *Looking down the corridors: Allied aerial espionage over East Germany and Berlin 1945–1990* Stroud: The History Press.

Wyden, P. H. 1989 *Wall: The inside story of divided Berlin* New York: Simon and Schuster.

Cartographic sources

Militairische situations karte von der gegend Berlin, Potsdam and Spandau E. W. Starck 1810.

Gross Berlin 1913 1.40 000 Bibliographisches Institut Leipzig.

Germany Allemagne Sheet 3 1944 3 US Army copied from a German map date 1937.

Gross-Berlin c1959 1.35 000 Falk-Verlag.

Gross-Berlin c1961 1.35 000 Falk-Verlag.

Richard Schware AG Berlin *U-Bahn netz* S W Sheet c1961.

Schaffman und Kluge *Stadtplan von Berlin* 1.20 000 S W Sheet c1961.

Gross-Berlin c1965 1.35 000 Falk-Verlag.

Schaffman und Kluge *Wanderkarte Wassersportkarteld Grunewald and Havelseen* 1.20 000 c1965.

Stadtplan von Gross-Berlin 1.35 000 Sehenswürdigkeiten c1965.

RV Reise-und Verkehrsverlag nd. 198? *Grosser Stadtplan Berlin* Berlin: RV Reise-und Verkehrsverlag.

Berlin and Potsdam 1983 1.25 000 1 of 4 Soviet army map.

Berlin and Potsdam 1983 1.25 000 3 of 4 Soviet army map.

Web sources

'Brian Patchett' www.langeleben.co.uk/Brian%20Patchett/brian_patchett_page1. htm accessed 07 01 16.

Der Tagesspiegel 2011 'Der Teufelsberg Die ruine lebt' www.tagesspiegel.de/berlin/ die-ruine-lebt/4174558.html accessed 31 10 15.

GoogleEarth www.google.co.uk/intl/en_uk/earth/ accessed 31 10 15.

http://ronbosoldier.blogspot.com/2005/12/history-and-pictures-of-us-army.html accessed 31 10 15.

'HQ, US Army Security Agency, Europe, (TAREX) Frankfurt-on-Main, West Germany: The end of my army career' www.cdstrand.com/areas/usasaeur.htm accessed 28 12 15.

'NSA field station Teufelsberg: A late post mortem' http://dasalte.ccc.de/teufelsberg accessed 31 10 15.

Pellington, R. L. nd 'My duty on "Spooky Hill"' www.berlin-brigade.de/honor/honor7.html#rob accessed 13 02 11 (no longer active).

Pilzak 2000 email 31 December www.fsbrg.homestead.com/history.htlml accessed 10 01 11(no longer active).

'RAF 646 Signals Unit' ww2.warwick.ac.uk/fac/soc/pals/staff/alrich/vigilant/lectures/gchq/646_su_memories_2.doc accessed 02 11 15.

Stache, M. 2000 email 30 April www.fsbrg.homestead.com/history.htlml accessed 10 01 11(no longer active).

v. Broenewski, R. nd 'Pre-history of T-berg' www.berlinbrigade.de/us-ins/us-rin16.html accessed 10 01 11.

www.birgelenvets.org/webpages/history.aspx   Birgelen   Veterans   Association accessed 31 10 15.

www.jao.delboys.com/26SU.htm 26 Signals Unit accessed 31 10 15.

www2.warwick.ac.uk/fac/soc/pais/people/aldrich/vigilant/lectures/gchq/646_su_memories_2.doc accessed 26 1 16.

Index

For Product Safety Concerns and Information please contact our EU
representative GPSR@taylorandfrancis.com
Taylor & Francis Verlag GmbH, Kaufingerstraße 24, 80331 München, Germany

www.ingramcontent.com/pod-product-compliance
Ingram Content Group UK Ltd.
Pitfield, Milton Keynes, MK11 3LW, UK
UKHW021425080625
459435UK00011B/161